NEW DIRECTIONS FOR PROGRAM EVALUATION
A Publication of the American Evaluation Association

William R. Shadish, *Memphis State University*
EDITOR-IN-CHIEF

Evaluation in the Federal Government: Changes, Trends, and Opportunities

Christopher G. Wye
National Academy of Public Administration

Richard C. Sonnichsen
U.S. Federal Bureau of Investigation

EDITORS

Number 55, Fall 1992

JOSSEY-BASS PUBLISHERS
San Francisco

EVALUATION IN THE FEDERAL GOVERNMENT:
CHANGES, TRENDS, AND OPPORTUNITIES
Christopher G. Wye, Richard C. Sonnichsen (eds.)
New Directions for Program Evaluation, no. 55
William R. Shadish, Editor-in-Chief

Microfilm copies of issues and articles are available in 16mm and 35mm, as well as microfiche in 105mm, through University Microfilms Inc., 300 North Zeeb Road, Ann Arbor, Michigan 48106.

LC 85-644749 ISSN 0164-7989 ISBN 1-55542-740-5

NEW DIRECTIONS FOR PROGRAM EVALUATION is part of The Jossey-Bass Education Series and is published quarterly by Jossey-Bass Inc., Publishers (publication number USPS 449-050).

EDITORIAL CORRESPONDENCE should be sent to the Editor-in-Chief, William R. Shadish, Department of Psychology, Memphis State University, Memphis, Tennessee 38152.

The paper used in this journal is acid-free and meets the strictest guidelines in the United States for recycled paper (50 percent recycled waste, including 10 percent post-consumer waste). Manufactured in the United States of America.

Instructions to Contributors

New Directions for Program Evaluation (NDPE), a quarterly sourcebook, is an official publication of the American Evaluation Association. As such, NDPE publishes empirical, methodological, and theoretical work on all aspects of program evaluation and related fields. Substantive areas may include any area of social programming such as mental health, education, job training, medicine, or public health, but may also extend the boundaries of evaluation to such topics as product evaluation, personnel evaluation, policy analysis, or technology assessment. In all cases, the focus on evaluation is more important than the particular substantive topic.

NDPE does not consider or publish unsolicited single manuscripts. Each issue of NDPE is devoted to a single topic, with contributions solicited, organized, reviewed, and edited by a guest editor. Issues may take any of several forms, such as a series of related chapters, a monograph, or a long article followed by brief critical commentaries. In all cases, proposals must follow a specific format that can be obtained from the Editor-in-Chief. These proposals are sent to members of the editorial board, and to relevant substantive experts, for peer review. This process may result in rejection, acceptance, or a recommendation to revise and resubmit. However, NDPE is committed to working constructively with potential guest editors to help them develop acceptable proposals. Close contact with the Editor-in-Chief is encouraged during proposal preparation and generation.

Copies of NDPE's "Guide for Proposal Development" and "Proposal Format" can be obtained from the Editor-in-Chief:

William R. Shadish, Editor-in-Chief
New Directions for Program Evaluation
Department of Psychology
Memphis State University
Memphis, Tennessee 38152
Office: 901-678-4687
FAX: 901-678-2579
Bitnet: SHADISHWR@MEMSTVX1

Contents

Editors' Notes

In 1988, the directors of the American Evaluation Association (AEA) appointed us co-chairs of the Ad Hoc Committee on the Status of Program Evaluation in the Federal Government. At the outset, we did not intend to produce a book, or report, or article. We began this activity not knowing exactly what to do and ended up with a variety of information, useful articles that we had come across, and essays that we had either written ourselves or invited others to write. It seemed logical to bring all of these sources together in one place for everyone, but particularly for members of AEA, to see. This book is not, however, an official report of the Ad Hoc Committee or of the board of directors but rather a collection of related chapters on a topical issue.

We learned along the way that not a great deal is known about evaluation among personnel in the federal government, or at least there is less known than one might reasonably expect. This limited knowledge characterizes evaluation practitioners in Washington as well as those in academe, private consulting, business, and other parts of the private sector.

Assuming that institutional evaluation is the largest single form of evaluation activity and that the federal government is the largest among the institutions using evaluation, we need to have a fair understanding of evaluation in the public sector if for no other reason than to understand who we are as a group of professionals. But there is also another reason to know more about evaluation in government. Today, when the country is facing an enormous imbalance between resources and needs, evaluation is a necessity. The public deserves not just smaller government (if that is what it decides to have) but efficient, effective, forward looking, innovative use of its tax dollars. If government is a public trust, then that trust carries a requirement for the highest level of performance—and improved performance is the aim of evaluation.

Four years ago, when we began our work, the state of evaluation in the federal government was not good. Today, depending on what part of the government is examined, it is in somewhat better condition. But in the social agencies—those agencies that administer social programs, such as the Departments of Health and Human Services, Labor, and Housing and Urban Development—evaluation is so minimal as to be a shadow of its earlier presence, and, in general, the *concept* of evaluation as an essential part of good management is simply not widely recognized.

Purpose and Organization

Our intent here is to report on the current status of program evaluation in the federal government by providing some sense of how evaluation is organized in the government: Who does it, why, and where? An obvious beginning is to describe evaluation in both the legislative and executive branches of government, and within each of these to review the major organizations producing evaluation work.

In choosing the organizations to include in the review, we relied on a broad definition of evaluation. In general, it is accurate to say that the functions described here are more "evaluative" than "evaluation" in nature. The criteria used to determine evaluative functions are that the activities be data based, involve analysis, and be objective. While this definition overstates evaluation capacity, it has the effect of better informing nonspecialists on the generic issue of information flow within and among the branches of government, a context in which any future evaluation activity must function. And, in particular, it highlights some of the key imbalances that must be overcome if the government is to have an adequate evaluation capacity.

A Note on Conceptual and Ideological Contexts

Before we outline the chapters in this volume, *Evaluation in the Federal Government: Changes, Trends, and Opportunities,* it is important to describe the conceptual and ideological contexts into which the idea of program evaluation currently must fit. For the last ten years, government policy has reflected a clear ideology about the role of government itself and about government programs—especially social programs. In a phrase, smaller is better. It is not necessary to accept or reject that ideology to understand the context and conditions of evaluation in the government today, but it is crucial to take the ideology into account.

During the same ten-year period, one conceptual issue in particular became extremely important to those interested in the performance of government and government programs. The overarching concept for improving government performance has been control: management control, internal control, fraud control, waste control. These are the names of some of the major management initiatives of the period. The essential concept is one of boundaries, limits, and even walls. Again, one need not take up the case for or against this approach to take into account its management consequences.

Both of these vectors on government operations—smaller is better and management by control—are considered in the chapters that follow. Both work against evaluation. If the purpose is to reduce the size of government, then it is effective and logical to reduce staff (support) functions before line (programs) functions. Certainly, the political fallout is going to be less. And if the purpose is to eliminate fraud, waste, and mismanagement, then control is an effective and logical way to proceed.

Only if the purpose is to improve government performance (of whatever size and shape) does the question change.

The Importance of Evaluation in Government

This volume, published as part of an association series for a specific evaluation audience, does not need to remind readers of the importance of evaluation. The three chapters in Part One are included not only because of what is said but because of when and by whom they were written. The statement by Charles A. Bowsher, the comptroller general of the United States, and the chapter by Elliott L. Richardson, former cabinet secretary in several departments of government, are exercises in courage and leadership. At a time when, in some areas of government, evaluation has not only been excised from the administrative process but become one of the least attractive causes in Washington, D.C., these statements present brief, compelling cases for the essential role of evaluation in government. They also offer comfort, heart, and hope for a better future.

In Chapter One, Bowsher, in his introduction to the General Accounting Office report *Program Evaluation Issues,* appeals to the interests of political appointees when he observes that information is essential in budget, management, and policy debate, and that if the executive agencies do not have their own internal evaluation capacity to generate it, then others will supply it. The question posed to political appointees in the executive branch is, "Wouldn't you rather have your own base for information to make your case?"

Chapter Two presents several pages from the introduction of *Program Evaluation Issues.* The point made is that executive branch program managers need program evaluations to do their jobs, and that if the executive branch does not produce its own evaluations, then the legislative branch will be forced to produce them.

To Richardson, in Chapter Three, the management of government programs without evaluation is inconceivable. Making the distinction often ignored by political appointees between output and outcome, he argues that we must be responsible not only for getting program services out to the public but also for ensuring that they achieve the intended result, not just for the delivery of services but for effective and efficient management of public dollars.

Evaluation in the Executive Branch: The Social Agencies

The chapters in Part Two focus attention on the social agencies in government because those agencies are where the reductions in evaluation capacity have been the most severe. But it needs to be said at the outset that the evaluation functions in other areas of the government have not suffered to the same degree. The federal government is such a vast organizational leviathan that in a number of areas evaluation functions have been little touched by recent trends. In fact, some are not only distant from recent budget and staffing trends but also from some of the newer approaches to evaluation that have emerged in the last fifteen years.

In Chapter Four, Harry S. Havens strongly states the case that evaluation has been virtually eliminated from the social agencies of the executive branch. While possibly overdrawn in the empirical sense (Are there or are there not evaluations?), his statement nevertheless rings true in the conceptual sense (Is there an understanding of the essential role of evaluation?). Havens concludes that evaluation must be rebuilt from the ground up.

Also of note in Havens's chapter is his comparison of the relative maturities of the fields of auditing and evaluation. Auditing, he points out, is widely accepted as an essential tool in government management, but auditors have had many decades in which to perfect techniques and management procedures. Evaluation, by contrast, has a history of less than twenty years. His point is that if in times past evaluation in the government was academic and not always as useful as it could have been, then we need to look at its stage of development and allow for growth. The client orientation of evaluation in recent years supports this view.

In Chapter Five, Eleanor Chelimsky summarizes the best empirical information available about the status of evaluation in the executive branch of the government. Based on information gathered by the Program Methodology and Evaluation Division of the General Accounting Office in 1980, 1984, and 1988, she demonstrates that evaluation in the executive branch has experienced substantial budget and staff cutbacks. The analysis also shows an increasing tendency of evaluation functions to conduct smaller studies and to address internal management issues rather than issues of program outcome and design.

The remaining three chapters in this section provide case studies of three basic trends in evaluation functions. In Chapter Six, Alan Ginsburg tells the story of an evaluation function that survived. Like many other evaluation offices, the Planning and Evaluation Service at the Department of Education went through a period of severe resource cutbacks. But through astute management and the use of creative methods, the office has been able to rebuild and even exceed its initial resource base and sphere of influence. Especially noteworthy in this case is the use of outside panels of independent experts to review evaluation reports for soundness and relevance. During the period when its budget and staff were declining, one of the major charges leveled against the office was that its work was not relevant or useful. The use of outside panels provided a quality review mechanism and a network of outside, professional support for quality evaluation work. Given that the internal constituency for evaluation work can rarely compete with that of the programs assessed, the development of an outside constituency offers one of the few routes open to evaluators seeking to broaden their base of support. It also offers a mechanism for getting good evaluation out of an agency and into public view, which is not always easy to accomplish.

In Chapter Seven, David B. Rymph discusses the experience of an evaluation office in the Department of Housing and Urban Development that was eliminated. Following a ten-year period of attrition, during which budget and staffing cutbacks were parried with adaptive approaches but decline continued, the evaluation office was reorganized as a policy coordination function. This pattern of transforming a policy analysis or evaluation function into a policy coordination activity is characteristic of the last decade of operations throughout the executive branch. The function of policy coordination has nothing to do with either analysis or evaluation. Its purpose is to ensure that existing or new policy conforms with the stated objectives of an organization. In effect, its activity is one of oversight. In day-to-day operation, much of its focus is on review of written material—from outgoing letters written by program managers to reports, memoranda, and speeches.

In Chapter Eight, Michael F. Mangano describes an emerging trend: the movement of inspector general functions toward evaluation work. In the federal government, each major department or agency has an inspector general whose major activity prior to the 1980s was to conduct program audits and legal investigations. In the last ten years, as increasing interest has been shown in controlling fraud, waste, and abuse, inspectors general have ridden a rising tide of staff and budget support as they have frequently been delegated responsibility for managing the various control initiatives of the period (management control, internal control, and fraud control). The legislation authorizing inspectors general enables them to do program evaluation work. Until the present decade, however, they had enough to do in terms of audit and investigative activity, and program evaluation needs were met by program evaluation units. But as the criticism of evaluation functions grew and their budget and staff resources declined, inspectors general stepped in to fill the void.

Mangano describes the development of the inspections function in the Office of the Inspector General at the Department of Health and Human Services. Mangano's office is the pacesetter in an area that is gaining attention for its useful work. The inspections function does not cover the full range of evaluation work, focusing less on long-term in-depth projects, but its practical approach to delivering useful evaluation products on time is gaining adherents. The issue for evaluators is the extent to which the movement of inspectors general toward evaluation broadens or narrows the application of evaluation methodologies to government programs. At the very least, the increasing tendency of inspectors general to do evaluation studies indicates that evaluators have not made the case for what they do clearly enough to support a separate identity for themselves. The line between audit and evaluation functions may be clear in theory, but in practice it has become blurred.

The Executive Branch: The Central Agencies

In the parlance of the federal government, three agencies are seen as so critical to the operation of the federal government that they are called "the central agencies." These include the Office of Management and Budget (OMB), the Office of Personnel Management (OPM), and the General Services Administration (GSA). They are discussed here, in part, to advance an understanding in the evaluation profession as to the kinds and locations of evaluation that take place in the government.

OMB prepares the president's budget and manages the executive branch portfolio of programs. Its interest in evaluation is more what we think of as evaluation: evaluation as a means to assess programs. Unlike the other central agencies, whose attitudes toward and use of program evaluation have relatively little effect on the use of program evaluation by other executive branch agencies, the posture of OMB toward executive branch evaluation is all but determining. As the keeper of the president's policy, management, and budget program, it plays an influential leadership role. In Chapter Nine, Christopher G. Wye traces OMB policy toward evaluation from the early 1980s to the present. This period might be characterized as encompassing the fall and rise of OMB interest in evaluation. As Wye shows, beginning in the early 1980s, OMB clearly withdrew its support for the use of evaluation activity and repeatedly reduced its budget and staffing resources in the departments and agencies of the executive branch. Since 1988, this direction has been reversed, and OMB has begun to articulate a clear understanding of the need for evaluation. But staff and budget support have not followed, so that at the end of four years during which OMB has supported the concept of evaluation, the social agencies remain in a depleted state in regard to their evaluation capacity.

So much evaluation is discussed in terms of its application to social programs that its use in many other areas is often overlooked. OPM is the central office in charge of managing governmentwide personnel policy and operations. It has a long tradition of evaluation in connection with the placement, rating, and promotion of government personnel. In Chapter Ten, Deborah Jordan discusses OPM's decades-long search for a workable balance between centralized and decentralized approaches to personnel management.

GSA also has an evaluation function to assess the government's management of its property—buildings, cars, military bases. But if the kinds of evaluation carried out here are different from those we encounter elsewhere, the cutbacks in budget and staff as well as the resulting narrowing of scope that have affected them are quite similar. In Chapter Eleven, Caleb Kriesberg describes an increasing tendency of GSA evaluation to be decentralized and to focus more sharply on management issues.

The Legislative Branch: An Organization for Every Need

Although it is hard to find a department or agency in the executive branch that is well equipped to do evaluations, just the reverse is true in the legislative branch of the federal government. Again, applying a definition of evaluation activities that subsumes a broad array of analytical approaches to evaluation, we can see that the legislative branch of government has a range of analytical support unknown in the executive branch. Not only is the range of support broader, but with it the legislative branch is far better able to draw independent conclusions. In fact, if our criteria for an evaluation function include data, analysis, and objectivity, then we can say that while the executive branch has a greater ability to collect data and the two branches have roughly the same responsibility to do analytical work, the ability to draw objective conclusions is greater in the legislative branch.

A detailed examination of the reasons for this greater capacity for independence among evaluation functions in the legislative branch is beyond the scope of the present discussion. But two important points must be noted here. First, the major analytical functions in the legislative branch are organizations that focus solely on data analysis. This means that the self-preservation of these organizations depends on their analytical work because that is their sole function. So when budget and staffing crunches come, they cannot trade off evaluation functions to preserve program functions. Second and even more important, each of these organizations has only one political appointee, and that political appointee has a term that does not end with a given presidential administration. In the executive branch, the ratio of career-to-political appointees varies from agency to agency, but rare indeed is the agency with only one political appointee. In general, unfortunately, professionalism, objectivity, and independence frequently occur in inverse proportion to the degree of balance between career and political staff.

Notwithstanding their greater insulation from political pressures, the evaluation functions of the legislative branch were not totally exempt from the pressures surrounding analytical work in the 1980s. Budget and staff reductions and other trends affecting the executive branch were also evident in the legislative branch, but to a far lesser extent. In general, the budgets of legislative functions were stable during this period, although in real dollar terms this translated to an actual decline. The General Accounting Office (GAO), Congressional Budget Office (CBO), and Congressional Research Service (CRS) saw rises in requests for work related to financial management. CBO reversed a 60 to 40 percent allocation of resources that initially favored program analysis to an allocation that favored financial analysis.

Among the analytical agencies supporting the legislative branch, GAO is preeminent in size, evaluation focus, and range of work. Alone among the analytical functions of the legislative branch, GAO actually expanded the proportion of its work focused on evaluation during the 1980s. As its name implies, GAO began its existence as an audit function. But over time its work was increasingly broadened, and in recent years audit and evaluation work have been done side by side. GAO's announced goal is to be an evaluation agency.

Although evaluation work may be done anywhere within the organization, GAO has a special unit headed by an assistant comptroller general devoted to evaluation. In Chapter Twelve, this unit, the Program Evaluation and Methodology Division, is discussed by Eleanor Chelimsky, the current head. This unit is one of the most professional evaluation units in the government in terms of staff skills, methodologies, and quality of work produced. In many ways it is a model for what should be available in the executive branch. GAO evaluations can include, as a given project may require, the collection of original data and the application of sophisticated analytical techniques, although, as Chelimsky points out, frequently the need is a short-term product based on extant data.

As discussed by Dawn W. De Vere in Chapter Thirteen, CBO concentrates mainly on cost estimates and cost-effectiveness and cost-benefit analyses. But half of its divisions are organized around major program areas in the government, and much of its work is essentially evaluative in nature. CBO has earned a reputation for independence and objectivity, qualities most frequently seen when, after the president transmits the federal budget to Congress, it routinely projects more realistic figures.

CRS prepares relatively short, quick turnaround background reports for congressional representatives and senators. Typically, as Barbara Poitras Duffy discusses in Chapter Fourteen, these reports provide background information in relation to subjects that have gained public attention. But senior CRS specialists are nationally recognized experts in their fields, and their work is highly regarded for its professionalism. The work of senior analysts ranges from quick advice on fast-breaking issues to book-length reports taking several years to produce. CRS does not collect original data and rarely employs the kinds of analytical methodologies used by evaluators.

The work of the Office of Technology Assessment (OTA) is, from the perspective of the evaluation profession, even less evaluative in nature. It does not collect original data. It does not employ methodologies. And it does not so much provide analysis as expert opinion. As Elizabeth A. Hildes describes in Chapter Fifteen, most of its reports summarize the views of experts brought together around particular issues. But the work of the office reflects a high degree of professionalism, and it engenders wide respect.

The analytical functions available to the legislative branch—GAO, CBO, CRS, and OTA—reflect varying degrees of evaluation capacity. This capacity ranges along a continuum from the GAO's collection of new empirical data and application of sophisticated methodologies to the OTA's reliance on expert opinion. But, taken together, this array of analytical functions gives the legislative branch a far greater evaluation capacity than is available to the executive branch. Chapter Sixteen presents the concluding pages of the GAO report *Program Evaluation Issues*, which call upon the executive branch to rebuild its evaluation capacity.

Today, there is a clear imbalance in the analytical and evaluation capacities of the executive and legislative branches of government. While the capacity of the executive branch has eroded, that of the legislative branch has grown. The question of whether there recently has or has not been an upturn in the executive branch pales in significance beside the issue raised by the question of balance and threshold capacity. For whatever improvement may be in progress in the evaluation functions of the executive branch, it occurs within a budgetary climate in which more extensive and greater reductions are seen as necessary across the board.

At this late date, the question remains, If the issue is how to have a more efficient and effective government, why is program evaluation, which has improved performance as its central mission, seen as expendable? The answer to this question will be incomplete until it is addressed by both evaluation critics and practitioners.

Christopher G. Wye
Richard C. Sonnichsen
Editors

CHRISTOPHER G. WYE *is director of policy coordination in the Office of Community Planning and Development, U.S. Department of Housing and Urban Development. He is presently on an intergovernmental personnel assignment at the National Academy of Public Administration where he is staff director for a project on improving government performance through monitoring and program evaluation.*

RICHARD C. SONNICHSEN *is deputy assistant director in the Federal Bureau of Investigation, in charge of the Office of Planning, Evaluation, and Audits. He is responsible for evaluating FBI investigative and administrative programs, strategic planning, and financial audits. He is also an adjunct faculty member at the University of Southern California, Washington Public Affairs Center. His evaluation interests are in the areas of internal organizational evaluation and the utilization of evaluation results.*

In November 1988, the comptroller general of the United States, Charles A. Bowsher, issued the report Program Evaluation Issues, *which documented a serious decline in program evaluation capacity in the federal government. Reproduced below is his letter transmitting the report to the executive and legislative branches of government. The letter is significant because it is an unusually clear and forceful—and rare—statement of the essential role of program evaluation in government.*

Transmittal Letter: *Program Evaluation Issues*

Charles A. Bowsher

U.S. General Accounting Office
Washington, D.C. 20548
Comptroller General of the United States
November 1988

The President of the Senate
The Speaker of the House of Representatives
The Director-Designate, Office of Management and Budget

This summary report is one of a series that addresses major policy, management, or program issues facing the new Congress and administration. The discussion of issues, the problems associated with each, and recommended actions are based on our work in the program evaluation area.

In this report, we are concerned with the government's continuing ability to develop, disseminate, and use sound information. Production of sound and timely information is one of the most critical functions of government. Program evaluation—along with supporting data collection—is one of the best means available for obtaining it. Yet with few exceptions, we have found that both program evaluation and data collection capabilities have been gravely eroded in the executive branch.

Officials in both executive and legislative branches need quality evalu-

---

This chapter is included as a transmittal letter in U.S. General Accounting Office, *Program Evaluation Issues*, November 1988 (GAO/OCG-89-8TR).

ation to help them reach sound judgments. Without this capability, executive branch policymakers are in a weak position to pursue their policy objectives with the Congress, to justify continuation of their programs, and to eliminate wasteful or unnecessary initiatives, because they lack supporting data.

The legislative branch continues to need program evaluation findings, whether or not the executive branch produces them. If the current drawdown in evaluation capabilities continues, reports from the GAO, its sister agencies, and from private sector analysts may become the only sources to which the Congress can turn for sound information to guide key decisions. The erosion of evaluation capability in the executive branch will not insulate agency programs from congressional oversight. On the contrary, lacking their own evaluations, agencies could find themselves excluded from meaningful participation in congressional decisions.

For executive agencies to preserve their proper role in policy and program implementation, four actions are needed: (1) rebuilding staff capacity, (2) providing dedicated resources for program evaluation and data collection, (3) setting priorities to ensure that information arrives when needed, and (4) ensuring honest, full reporting, both to agency policymakers and to the Congress.

CHARLES A. BOWSHER *is comptroller general of the United States. As such, he is the senior executive in charge of the General Accounting Office, the largest analytical function in the legislative branch of the federal government.*

The General Accounting Office transition report to the executive and legislative branches of government, Program Evaluation Issues, *began with this short statement of the importance of evaluation in government.*

Why Program Evaluation Is Important

General Accounting Office

"The Department doesn't have anything on that" is rarely an acceptable answer by federal officials to questions about their programs, yet that is a statement heard with increasing regularity. We do not minimize the difficulties of determining program effectiveness. We do emphasize that there are proven methods for getting credible answers to questions about program operation and effectiveness. These methods collectively are called program evaluation.

When an Iranian airliner is shot down by an Aegis missile in the Persian Gulf, or when Wall Street goes into economic meltdown, the call for information comes loud and clear. Less dramatic, but equally real, are the "routine" demands for data on how effectively the federal government is using its trillion-dollar plus budget. In 1988, for example, federal officials testified several thousand times before Congress and provided over 3,000 legislatively required reports, according to agency estimates. At the least, these reports should provide relevant, timely, and technically adequate data on federal programs.

Program evaluation—when it is available and of high quality—provides sound information about what programs are actually delivering, how they are being managed, and the extent to which they are effective or cost-effective. Unfortunately, we have discovered through our surveys that program evaluation and the data collection that supports it are—with few exceptions—in a depleted state in executive agencies today. Further, case studies show that basic data are lacking on such disparate and wide-ranging

---

This chapter is from U.S. General Accounting Office, *Program Evaluation Issues,* November 1988 (GAO/OCG-89-8TR).

issues as health care quality, the state of the environment, and the results of weapon system testing. This shortage of evaluative information should be of immediate concern to federal managers; they need it both to run their programs and to justify their decisions and performance. It is certainly of concern to GAO; it means a corresponding overflow in requests to us for information on program results. But the most important point is that the shortage is really everyone's concern, because good information is not just a management tool. It is the responsibility of government to the people of this country, and it is not in a healthy state.

In the past, sound evaluations have contributed strongly to well-informed decisions, such as those to maintain effective programs like Head Start or Runaway and Homeless Youth. Without such evaluations, these important programs might not have survived the budget cuts that depleted other programs whose effectiveness had not been so solidly established. Also, in the past, programs such as the breeder reactor or binary chemical weapons have been dropped or slowed down because evaluations convincingly showed their extreme weakness. Today, however, the capability to perform program evaluation is drying up, not the least in such areas as defense, health care, education, and the environment, where it is precisely most needed.

Evaluation is an essential part of government administration. Scarce public resources need to be used in the most efficient and effective manner. This necessity was never more pressing than today, when the country faces a growing list of unmet social needs.

The Value of Evaluation

Elliott L. Richardson

When I spoke recently on the urgent need to rebuild the public service, I drew the contrast between today and those earlier times when people came to Washington in hopes of bettering the lives of their fellow Americans. A major goal of the New Deal, after all, was to address the galaxy of human needs that, until that time, had been neglected at all levels of government. The same drive manifested itself later in the Fair Deal, the Great Society, and the War on Poverty. To be a part of any of these efforts was to experience a sense of idealism and service, a feeling that government was undertaking experiments that would challenge its capacity to better some of the most keenly felt deficiencies in American society.

But the problem with these efforts was that while they substantially reshaped the role of government, they eventually generated a level of expectation that they could never fulfill. This was a matter that deeply concerned me when I became secretary of Health, Education, and Welfare (HEW) in 1970, early in the Nixon administration. At the time, HEW was still geared toward establishing bigger and better programs to respond to a host of unmet social needs. But it became very apparent to me, even in the first months following my arrival, that we were overpromising. I tried frequently to convince my colleagues at HEW that we would eventually need to choose among the many claims on our limited resources, and that in order to do so with some measure of rationality, we would need to focus far more

---

Originally based on a speech presented at the 8th annual GAO Management Conference in Chantilly, Virginia, on November 28, 1990, this chapter is reprinted with permission with minor revisions from the *GAO Journal*, Spring 1991, pp. 37–41.

than we had been doing on identifying the programs that actually improved people's lives.

There is a way of dramatizing just how limited our resources were at that time. I asked my staff late in 1971 to estimate how much it would cost in fiscal year 1972 to extend all of HEW's service delivery programs—there were 308 at the time—to every eligible person. It turned out that the additional cost for fiscal year 1972 alone would have been $250 billion, enough to double not the HEW budget but the year's entire federal budget. The expanded programs, moreover, would have required the recruitment and training of at least twenty million new service providers and administrators.

The resources of the federal government, in relative terms, are certainly no greater now than then. Today, the government faces the challenge of overcoming the disillusionment that followed in the wake of overinflated hopes and expectations. Beyond that, moreover, it must also struggle simply to keep from being overwhelmed by its responsibilities—responsibilities, it must be noted, that no other level of government is any better equipped to fulfill. The list of demands and unmet needs is long and depressing.

I daresay that there have been General Accounting Office (GAO) reports addressing every one of these issues and many more equally urgent ones: cleaning up toxic waste, softening the blow of catastrophic illness, ensuring air safety, deterring insider trading, containing terrorism, holding down the escalation of health care costs, restricting nuclear hazards, combating the AIDS pandemic, promoting competitiveness, fighting drug abuse, overcoming the trade imbalance, dealing with the savings and loan mess, coping with the social strains consequent to the emergence of the social underclass, helping welfare mothers find work, and so on.

If this daunting array of problems is to receive any effective response, it can come only through the most efficient possible use of the government's limited political, managerial, and fiscal capacities. Only rarely these days do we find ourselves caught up in the old debates—such as those that swirled around the New Deal—over the appropriateness of federal involvement in such issues. There is no conservative of my acquaintance who would deny that this nation faces significant problems, and hardly any who would not say that these problems deserve government concern and response. The question has become not whether to respond but *how* to respond—how to apply the government's resources as effectively as possible to new demands while continuing to address the many issues that cannot simply be lopped off the agenda.

As soon as we begin to talk about the need for improving the government's capacity to choose among competing claims on its limited resources, we return inevitably to the matter of rebuilding the public service. Adequate responses to the spectrum of competing claims will require that the federal government replenish its human and intellectual capital. The government needs people who are familiar with the available means of addressing these problems and who have the ability to design and manage programs that make the most precise, surgical use of these means. We cannot afford any longer to intervene clumsily in society's problems, and then intervene again to correct the mistakes made the first time around. We thus have greater need than ever before for people in government who have a profound understanding of the interrelationships among government organizations; the interrelationships among government and private-sector entities, both voluntary and for profit; the techniques of intervention; the processes of management; and the means of ensuring accountability.

This need for the best possible people is axiomatic. A corollary, however, is that those in government must become more involved in the same pursuit toward which I urged my colleagues at HEW, and in which GAO has become so usefully engaged in recent years; that of ensuring not just that government agencies are devoting their resources to the purposes for which they were created but also that these resources are actually accomplishing the goals with which the agencies have been charged. At the heart of this pursuit is rigorous evaluation. As I wrote nearly fifteen years ago (Richardson, 1976, p. 138), in the absence of rigorous evaluation, "We cannot . . . find out how well—or how poorly—a particular effort is succeeding. And only if we know this—and know also the effectiveness of an alternative approach to the same objective—can we compare the two. Only thus, moreover, can we judge the value of pursuing the objective at all versus that of devoting the same resources to some wholly different purpose."

It is true, of course, that attempts at evaluation have always been subject to certain weaknesses, some of which grew out of the widespread reliance on contractors to do the evaluating. In Richardson (1976), I sympathized with the feeling that too large a share of the money spent on evaluation, like that spent on research, went to the sort of contractor whose only visible qualification was a staff of ex-employees of the contracting agency. I mentioned a more basic weakness, however: the typical contracting agency's own inability to define with precision what it wanted to have evaluated, and then to monitor the contractor's performance of the defined task.

Another problem I pointed out, and one I suspect is still encountered today, is that attempts at evaluation were often simply directed at whatever Congress had called a "program," even though the program might, in fact, involve a whole array of activities, such as formula grants to state and local governments, project grants to nonprofit organizations, and support of training programs. Attempts at evaluation addressed to this kind of bureaucratic laundry list are seldom very useful.

But in an era in which the limited resources of the federal government are stretched to the breaking point, the most serious weakness in evaluation may be the instinct of the evaluator, particularly the internal evaluator, to apply input measures rather than to find out if the activity under evaluation is actually accomplishing anything. For example, I remember the time when, as attorney general, I was invited to New York City to dedicate the new police headquarters. I was met at the airport by a deputy commissioner who was responsible for the city's battle against organized crime. I asked him how he was doing. "Great," he said. "Really?" I said. "What have you done?" He recounted the number of people that he had sent to jail. I said, "That's fine. But has that had any effect on organized crime?" He continued in the same vein, telling me about the various indictments that he had obtained and the dent made in the Colombo gang—or whatever—and how the New York Police Department now had the Mafia on the run. I said, "That's also fine. But have your efforts reduced any of the activities in which organized crime is engaged? Is there any less illegal gambling?" He looked at me quizzically and asked, "What does that have to do with it? We're fighting organized crime."

This reminiscence brings us back to something I mentioned earlier, something GAO has understood for quite a long time. It is not enough simply to ensure that funds are spent on the purposes for which they were appropriated, or that people are carrying out their assigned tasks. The real question is whether, by doing these things, the agency is actually achieving its objectives.

While I was at HEW, I visited GAO to talk about evaluation with Elmer Staats. As I later wrote, "Now, under the leadership of Comptroller General Elmer B. Staats, who serves as Congress's watchdog over federal spending, [GAO is] making it a routine practice also to look into the efficacy of the expenditure. As Mr. Staats remarked in a recent address, 'From where we sit, it appears that both the executive and legislative branches of our government have been more concerned with starting new programs than with making certain that those we already have are working satisfactorily or could be improved.' "

GAO has, of course, made further strides since then. I recently saw an article by Eleanor Chelimsky (1990) in which she reviewed the history of evaluation at GAO, focusing on the creation in the 1970s—about the time of my conversations with Staats—of the Program Analysis Division, and then the creation of the Institute for Program Evaluation in 1980, followed by its redesignation as the Program Evaluation and Methodology Division in 1983.

Unfortunately, at about the same time that GAO's new division was created, the data gathering and analytical functions of the entire executive branch began falling into neglect. This was a matter of so much concern to me at the start of the Reagan administration that I went to see David Stockman, then director of the Office of Management and Budget (OMB). I tried to persuade him that no more serious damage could be done to the capacity of the government to make intelligent policy and programmatic choices than to allow the data base to decay. Nevertheless, that decay is exactly what happened. In a transition report, GAO (1988, p. 7) called attention to the serious deterioration of these key functions of the federal government: "Unfortunately, we have discovered through our surveys that program evaluation and the data collection that supports it are—with few exceptions—in a depleted state in executive agencies today. Further, case studies show that basic data are lacking on such disparate and wide-ranging issues as health care quality, the state of the environment, and the results of weapon system testing." The report went on to state that "in 1984, and again in 1988, a review of evaluation services in non-Defense agencies found a significant general decline since 1980 in the capacity and availability of data on federal programs, although agencies varied" (GAO, 1988, p. 9).

This report is troubling to look back on, particularly when you recall that, even at its best, evaluation of federal programs was simply not that good. Fortunately, there has been a turnaround during Bush's administration—if not in results, at least in attitude. GAO (1990) published a discussion paper in May 1990, titled *Improving Program Evaluation in the Executive Branch*. The preface notes that in a meeting with GAO staff in May 1989, OMB officials agreed with the GAO analysis of the problem and the seriousness of the situation. The OMB officials asked GAO to detail what OMB could do to improve things, focusing on long-term institutional changes rather than on the short-term fixes, but still assuming only a limited increase in staffing or funding.

We may take further encouragement from the director of OMB, Richard G. Darman. He spoke before the Council for Excellence in Government, delivering a speech with the rather Darmanesque title of "Neo-Neo-ism: Reflections on Hubble-ism, Rationalism, and the Pursuit of Excellence (After the Fiscal Follies)" (Darman, 1990). Darman makes a persuasive case that, as a result of the recent five-year budget legislation, the requirement for intelligent choices among competing policies and programs will be felt more urgently than ever before. The new sequester process, strengthened with spending caps, minisequesters, and "pay-as-you-go" requirements, bears him out. But while the new budgetary framework compels hard choices, it provides us with the opportunity to take a fresh look at a host of issues, such as the changing distribution of government benefits by age and income class, the shift from future-oriented investment programs toward present-oriented income transfers, the relative emphasis on prevention versus treatment, and the opportunity for expansion of empowering, market-oriented programs.

Darman's tongue is in his cheek, of course, when he uses the term *neo-neo-ism* to take a jab at the New Deal, the New Frontier, and the "new paradigm." But on a more serious level, he notes that we have a number of opportunities to combine the best of "both the romantic rush of Neo-ism and the rationalist interest in systematic progress." One of these opportunities—he identifies five—is the extensive evaluation of both federal programs and "natural," nonfederal experiments.

Evaluation fell out of favor as the federal initiatives of the 1960s and 1970s proved disappointing and early attempts at evaluation were shown to be flawed or biased. But systematic and sustained investment in evaluation is essential if intellectual capital is to be increased and if wisdom is to be gained from what would otherwise be fleeting facts.

We must do our best to hold the budget director to his commitment. I think what he says about the role of the 1990 budget legislation in exerting this kind of pressure is undoubtedly valid. It could, in fact, shift the emphasis of governing from the older route of identifying new needs and implementing new programs to the newer one of improving our capacity to meet existing needs.

If this shift does occur, it will, of course, put additional pressure on GAO. But it will also give GAO added reason both to continue coaching OMB in the art of evaluation and to remind OMB that the "m" in its title does not yet deserve a capital letter. Meanwhile, it will make it more important than ever for GAO to promote a higher level of evaluation throughout the federal government and, more broadly, to encourage a higher level of maturity among the American people, who need to accept the necessity of making choices.

References

Chelimsky, E. "Expanding GAO's Capabilities for Program Evaluation." *GAO Journal*, Winter-Spring 1990, pp. 37–42.

Darman, R. G. "Neo-Neo-ism: Reflections on Hubble-ism, Rationalism, and the Pursuit of Excellence (After the Fiscal Follies)." Paper presented at the Council for Excellence in Government, Washington, D.C., November 16, 1990.

General Accounting Office. *Program Evaluation Issues*. GAO/OCG-89-8TR. Washington, D.C.: Government Printing Office, 1988.

General Accounting Office. *Improving Program Evaluation in the Executive Branch*. GAO/PEMD-90-19. Washington, D.C.: Government Printing Office, 1990.

Richardson, E. L. *The Creative Balance: Government, Politics, and the Individual in America's Third Century*. Troy, Mo.: Holt, Rinehart & Winston, 1976.

ELLIOTT L. RICHARDSON is former secretary of Health, Education, and Welfare, secretary of the Department of Defense, attorney general of the United States, secretary of the Department of Commerce, and ambassador to the Court of Saint James. Currently, he is senior resident partner in the Washington office of Milbank, Tweed, Hadley, and McCloy. He is also a member of the Comptroller General's Consultant Panel and chair of the GAO Quality Control Review Board.

Program evaluation has been all but eliminated from government as a normal part of program management and needs to be rebuilt. Although early evaluation efforts can be criticized as costly, time-consuming, and in need of clearer focus, critics overlook the fact that evaluation is a relatively new profession and will require time to develop a solid place in public management.

The Erosion of Federal Program Evaluation

Harry S. Havens

It is an article of faith among professional public administrators that knowledge is a good thing. The more that we know about how our programs are functioning, effects they are having, and at what cost, the more likely we are to search out ways of making them more efficient and more effective. To a substantial degree, this knowledge is the public-sector manager's surrogate for the profit-and-loss statement of the business sector. But the information about costs, outputs, and effects needed by the public-sector manager does not emerge automatically, any more than corporate financial statements are self-generating. It took the accounting profession many decades to develop the rules, procedures, and systems that are the foundations of today's corporate financial reporting. Rigorous program evaluation in the public sector is a much younger function, a product at least on the civilian side of government, of the last twenty years or so. Thus, program evaluation is much less firmly established as an essential part of any public-sector operating agency and is inherently more fragile than is the accounting function in the private sector. This fragility is a key factor. It is inconceivable that a major public corporation today could suddenly decide to abolish its accounting function or to stop issuing financial statements. Such action would be a recipe for corporate suicide (and would be blatantly illegal). Yet something

The opinions expressed in this chapter are those of the author and do not necessarily represent or reflect the positions of the General Accounting Office. This chapter is reprinted, with permission, with minor revisions from *American Review of Public Administration,* 1990, *20* (1), 1–6.

very much akin to this action happened to program evaluation in the federal government during the 1980s.

The need for systematic, rigorous assessments of programs, particularly of their costs and effects, came to be generally recognized in the 1960s. The marriage of this need with disciplined analytical frameworks, first of economics and then of the other social sciences, was probably inevitable, given the intellectual orientations of the Kennedy and Johnson administrations. Although first manifest in Robert MacNamara's approach to managing the Defense Department, program analysis and evaluation soon was relegated (with some help from the top) to the civil agencies, where the most hospitable environment was found in the social program agencies, especially the Department of Health, Education, and Welfare and the Office of Economic Opportunity.

In retrospect, this sequence of development may have been unfortunate because of the connotations that came to be attached to program evaluation in the social program agencies. In Defense, evaluation had the aura of a hard-nosed business approach to ensuring accountability for program efficiency and effectiveness; it somehow lost this image in the social agencies. Instead, it came under attack by ideologues at both ends of the political spectrum. Some conservatives perceived that the evaluation process in the social agencies was a bunch of pointy-headed liberal intellectuals practicing social engineering. The fact that program evaluators, regardless of personal political leanings, have been among the most severe critics of the design and implementation of many social programs did not alter that impression. But hostility to rigorous program evaluation was not limited to those on the right of the political spectrum. Liberals often have been equally reluctant to see their pet programs subjected to careful examination, even when it was patently obvious that evaluation was an essential step in making those programs work well.

The lesson of this is that strong ideology, of any sort, is often the enemy of analysis. Those who fervently believe that they know the "truth" find facts inconvenient. Similarly, those who have a stake in a program can feel threatened by questions about effectiveness. These attitudes were the foundation for what happened to program evaluation at the federal level in the 1980s. Two data points developed by the U.S. General Accounting Office (GAO) through surveys of federal agencies help describe that experience. One survey (General Accounting Office, 1982) was conducted in 1980, with results reported in 1982. The other (General Accounting Office, 1987) was conducted in 1984 and reported in 1987. Subsequently, GAO reevaluated the issue as part of its Transition Series (General Accounting Office, 1988). Although GAO did not replicate the full survey for this latter report, evidence from a survey of fifteen agencies and from GAO's other work, most notably its general management reviews of major agencies, led GAO to conclude that the patterns observed in the 1984 survey had not changed.

What were these patterns? GAO started by simply looking at the number of units performing program evaluations. In 1980, 180 units in non-Defense agencies reported that they were engaged in program evaluation activities. By 1984, this figure was down to 133, which was not just an illusion reflecting consolidation or reorganization. The resources devoted to program evaluation were down as well. Measured in constant dollars, spending was down 37 percent and professional staff resources were down 22 percent. In some important areas, the shift from categorical to block grants was accompanied by a dramatic decline in evaluation effort. This pattern may seem reasonable on the surface. After all, with block grants, the federal government may have very little to say about the shape of the program to be funded at the state level. But that is a shortsighted view. The fact that a program has been shifted to other levels of government for implementation does not imply that the federal government, that Congress in particular, has lost interest in how the money is being spent and with what effect. To the contrary, following the shift to block grants, there was and remains a continuing flow of requests for GAO to assess what is happening to particular programs at the state and local levels. GAO can answer these questions, and it should be noted that most GAO reports on these issues are quite complimentary of the way that the states have handled their responsibilities. But in the broad scheme of things, it would be much better if the federal agencies responsible for the programs could provide credible answers. The erosion of agency evaluation capability has made that much less possible.

Two other things of considerable importance have been lost in the process. One is the ability to put together anything approaching a nationally representative picture of what is happening with problems that at least were once viewed as being of national significance. The other is the ability to assess rigorously, from a national perspective, samples of projects addressing similar problems. These losses have made it difficult both to judge how well the nation is responding to those problems and to share the lessons learned (both successes and failures) across jurisdictional boundaries.

The erosion of federal evaluation capability has been accompanied by a loss of national-level data. When the block grants were put in place, many of the former reporting requirements were eliminated. The resulting information gap has not been filled, perhaps accounting for a good portion of the purely informational audit requests that GAO receives from Congress. To some extent, of course, the erosion of federal data collection and evaluation capability can be, and has been, offset by a growing capacity at the state level. To those who are concerned about the quality of knowledge as the basis for decision making, the growing strength of state evaluation units and their colleagues in the academic research community is a gratifying trend.

Important as this development is, however, it can never fill more than part of the void at the federal level, just as no more than part of the void can be filled by GAO. State evaluation units are properly concerned primarily with issues affecting policy-making and program implementation within that state. Sharing the results of that work across state boundaries can be very useful. For example, the reports of state auditors and evaluators often contain valuable insights that are relevant to GAO's work. But information sharing makes only a modest contribution to the building of a reliable picture of national conditions that is needed by policymakers in the federal government. There is little incentive for state evaluators to join together in the coordinated studies needed to build such a mosaic. Many academic researchers are inclined to deal with the national picture but face a different problem. Few researchers have the resources to collect new data on a nationally representative sample. Most are dependent on existing data; the portion of this data collected by federal agencies in carrying out their programs can thus be very important. Thus, the research community, too, can fill only part of the void.

Another dimension of the problem is that there has been an unfortunate shift in the nature of the work being done in the agency evaluation units and in the audience for that work. Historically, the work has usually involved a mix of major studies on complex issues of program effectiveness, resulting in widely disseminated public reports and in smaller studies, often focused on narrower issues of program management and implementation, with results intended for an audience internal to the department or agency. Both sorts of work are needed, but for very different purposes.

The major studies, in particular, are a key to detecting and correcting flaws in existing program design that may undermine effectiveness or produce adverse side effects and to developing effective new programs in response to emerging problems. However, precisely this type of study has suffered most in the erosion of federal evaluation capacity. GAO's 1984 survey (GAO, 1987) established that as resources declined, the major studies were cut out. Subsequent evidence has confirmed the trend. As a result, a dramatically higher share of the declining resources is being devoted to short-term management studies that although important in their own right, can never provide reliable answers to key questions of program effectiveness.

Given this rather bleak picture of the current state of program evaluation in federal agencies, it is natural to ask what the implications of that situation are and what should be done about it. For better or worse, the policy process goes on with or without program evaluation. Congress, at least, will make decisions based on whatever information it can find. The same is true in the executive branch. Decisions will be made because they must be made. But the dearth of agency evaluation information will affect those decisions in two ways.

First, to the extent that the information gap cannot be filled from other sources such as GAO, state evaluation units, and the research community, there will be less basis for confidence in the resulting decisions. In view of the huge budget deficits, money cannot be wasted on ineffective programs, but that will be one of the results of shortchanging the investment in evaluation. Second, the loss of evaluation capacity means that agencies will lose some of the power to control their own destinies. When Congress makes policy, it listens to those who have something to say. Those who bring relevant and reliable information to the policy-making process often find that they have disproportionate influence on the outcome. In contrast, an agency that responds to substantive questions with nothing more than opinion, ideological rhetoric, or an acknowledgment of ignorance may well find itself ignored or totally excluded from decisions in which it has a vital interest. That result is unhealthy for the agency and for the policy-making process. Congress needs its own sources of information, but it does not need, and should not want, a monopoly on the relevant information. The wisest policies are likely to emerge from open and vigorous debate on the issues, with all sides arguing on the bases of reliable information to examine issues from different perspectives.

Where, then, do we go from here? The responsibility for rebuilding the government's program evaluation capacity and for using that capacity effectively rests with the executive branch and, more particularly, with the leadership of the operating agencies of government. Evaluation capacity will not be created and maintained unless the agency leadership wants that capacity, is prepared to invest in its creation, demands high-quality work, and uses the results of that work. Once that threshold is crossed, the actions needed to build a first-rate evaluation shop are easy to describe but much more difficult to implement. The ingredients are money, staff resources, time, and continued commitment from the top. High-quality program evaluation costs money; the more difficult and complex the questions, the more expensive the answers. But evaluation is cheap compared to the expense that occurs when money is wasted in a program with a flawed design, and the investment in evaluation is never wasted unless the work is shoddy or the results are ignored.

High-quality evaluation also requires talented people, and those people are not easily found. The universities, particularly in the graduate programs, are producing substantial numbers of people with the technical training appropriate for this work. As GAO has learned over the past couple of decades, however, technical training, although necessary, is not sufficient. To be effective, one must also understand and respect the political environment in which the work must be done, an environment that differs greatly from the academic community and that often defines words such as "important," "meaningful," and "relevant" in very different ways. Some elements of an understanding of that environment can be taught in the classroom, but most can be gained only from experience on the job.

Those seeking to build evaluation capacity also need to find managerial talent. As with any organization, an evaluation unit must be managed, and two factors make the management task especially challenging. The first factor is the government's established pattern of relying on outside contractors for the conduct of many major studies. Unless this pattern changes (and there is no reason to expect it), evaluation units must have the ability to manage large research contracts as well as the ability to conduct research directly. The second factor is the interdisciplinary character of the best evaluation research and the best evaluation units. No single discipline has a monopoly on insight into how to measure program effects. But as anyone who has tried it can attest, the task of managing an interdisciplinary team is tough. For example, the absence of a common language and a common frame of reference can cause enormous problems. It is easy to forget that different disciplines, such as accounting, economics, and budgeting, often use the same words but with very different meanings. These problems can be overcome with time and effort, but it takes a very skilled manager to work through them successfully, building strength out of diversity.

The last ingredient in rebuilding evaluation capacity is that the head of the agency and the top leadership team must demand high-quality evaluation, must insist that the results be reported honestly and objectively, both within and outside the agency, and must then use those results in the decision process. Rhetorical commitment alone is a waste of energy. Competent evaluators quickly recognize the manipulation of a study or a report to serve partisan or ideological purposes. The best evaluators will leave out of frustration and to avoid the stain on their professional reputations. Others may stay, but a pattern of manipulating results means that the credibility of any work (and of those producing it) is automatically suspect.

Can the erosion of federal evaluation capacity be reversed in view of these considerations? Of course it can. The hurdles are not insurmountable. We built the capacity from scratch once, and we can build it again. Will we do it? That is an open question. The most promising evidence is symbolic: the absence of the rigidly ideological and anti-analytical tone and rhetoric that were so common in many departments and agencies during the decade of the 1980s. In addition, conversations between GAO officials and senior officials of the present administration frequently have elicited statements from the latter acknowledging the need to rebuild the capacity for competent program evaluation and policy analysis. At that point, however, the commitment is only rhetorical. Meaningful action is yet to come. For example, the president's proposed budget for 1991 does not reveal any systematic effort to restore resources for the analytical units that were depleted in the 1980s.

In the long run, there is some basis for cautious optimism, stemming from an expectation that the leadership of the executive branch, the president, his close advisers, and the Cabinet will come to see that they cannot afford to lack a good evaluation capacity. In the policy-making process, which, after all, is central to presidential leadership, rhetoric and ideology can only carry one so far. In the end, victory goes to the side with the most convincing arguments. Reliable facts and solid analysis do not always win the day, but they sure help.

References

General Accounting Office. *A Profile of Federal Evaluation Activities.* GAO/IPE Special Study. Washington, D.C.: Government Printing Office, 1982.

General Accounting Office. *Federal Evaluation: Fewer Units, Reduced Resources, Different Studies from 1980.* GAO/PEMD-87-9. Washington, D.C.: Government Printing Office, 1987.

General Accounting Office. *Program Evaluation Issues.* GAO/OCG-89-8TR. Washington, D.C.: Government Printing Office, 1988.

HARRY S. HAVENS is assistant comptroller general of the United States, General Accounting Office.

General Accounting Office studies have documented a serious decline in executive branch evaluation capacity, as reflected in declining budget and staff resources and a narrowing of the methods employed and issues examined. However, increasing interest by the Office of Management and Budget and recent steps taken to encourage program evaluation should lead to its broader application and more frequent use.

Executive Branch Program Evaluation: An Upturn Soon?

Eleanor Chelimsky

The U.S. General Accounting Office (GAO) has, over time, described serious and apparently increasing problems with executive branch program evaluation capabilities. There currently is hope, however, for arresting this decline.

Importance of the Evaluation Function

Why does GAO believe that evaluation capabilities are important and that their decline is worth signaling to the president, the Congress, and the American public? There are essentially five reasons. First, the production of accurate and timely information, in general, is a truly basic function of any democratic government, and program evaluation is one of the best available means for producing it. Second, credible information about the value of what is being obtained in return for citizens' tax dollars helps to sustain public confidence in the national government. Third, policymakers and program managers must have systematic information from program evaluation, not only to help them make sound decisions about policies and programs in the midst of often ferocious political pressures but also to demonstrate their own public accountability. Fourth, in any top-priority

---

The opinions expressed in this chapter are those of the author and do not necessarily represent or reflect the positions of the General Accounting Office. This chapter is reprinted, with permission, with minor revisions from *The Bureaucrat,* 1990, *19* (3), 9-12.

area for both the Congress and the administration—the federal deficit, for example—program evaluation is the quintessential tool for determining the effectiveness of past policies and programs and for deciding where best to cut spending and to invest for the future. Fifth, evaluation not only permits good information to be produced but also deters production of bad information. That is, over the long term, a vigorous evaluation function whose independence is guaranteed and whose practitioners are technically competent will expose false, tendentious, or blatantly self-interested information and eventually preclude the production of at least some of it. If evaluation cannot always produce good decisions, it certainly can prevent decisions that either lack supporting data altogether or are based on data that have been egregiously manipulated.

Declining Capability

Unfortunately, despite all the good reasons invoked for maintaining a strong program evaluation capability in government, we at GAO have found that, in general, federal program evaluation is not in good health. After tracking the executive branch evaluation investment for a decade, we found that the overall situation (with some exceptions) entails less attention to strong, data-supported information (especially information about program or policy effectiveness), less concern with public accountability and public scrutiny, and a general downgrading of the evaluation function.

While some evaluation units are healthier than others (and some evaluators have as much work as they can handle), the overall data show large declines in funds spent on program evaluation as well as in the number of evaluation staff, along with a radical shift in the kind of information being produced. In this chapter, I report the GAO (1988) survey results that have led to these conclusions, illustrate the kind of information that is not available on crucial questions of public interest, and summarize our recommendations for revitalizing the federal evaluation function. In addition, I detail results of our work that seem to promise, if not a turnaround, at least some improvement in the presently bleak situation.

Evaluation Staff

Between 1980 and 1984, the number of professional staff in all federal agency evaluation units decreased by 22 percent, from about fifteen hundred to about twelve hundred. In contrast, the total number of staff in these agencies decreased by only 6 percent during this period. Particularly among the new units, evaluation staff were likely to come from management-oriented fields (such as business administration) rather than from the social sciences, which usually provide the technical training needed for sound research (such as knowledge about threats to validity and how to design studies to avoid these threats). Reductions in evaluation staff continued between 1984 and 1988. The fifteen agencies most active in 1980 experienced a 52 percent decline in evaluation staff between that year and 1988: down from 419 to 200.

Funds

Between 1980 and 1984, funds for program evaluation were reduced by 37 percent (in constant 1980 dollars) compared to a 4 percent increase for the agencies as a whole. Studies funded through legislative set-asides were somewhat less affected (27 percent reduction) than were those funded through internal budgets determined by the agencies themselves (40 percent reduction). The bottom line is that by 1984, only about $111 million across all non-Defense agencies were being spent on evaluation. What is the "right" amount differs, of course, among programs and observers. The point here is that, in the aggregate, this sum of $111 million had to cover the assessment of all domestic programs—a budget in the multiple billions of dollars. The precipitious decline in funding between 1980 and 1984 has abated in the past four years. This stability is partially due to the fact that legislative set-asides accounted for roughly 60 percent of the total resources allocated in 1984 and in 1988. By contrast, in 1980, 40 percent of the funds were derived from this source.

Significance of These Declines

Despite the decreases in staff and funds between 1980 and 1984 (22 percent and 37 percent, respectively), the number of evaluation studies decreased by only 3 percent across all federal non-Defense agencies. During this same time, the fifteen agencies surveyed in 1980 experienced a 48 percent decline in the number of studies. Part of the reduction for these agencies was offset, however, by a 19 percent increase in the number of studies between 1984 and 1988—despite an additional 20 percent loss of staff and roughly comparable loss of funding.

The impression of greater efficiency—the same or more work with fewer resources—is misleading. The same work was not being done in either 1984 or 1988 as had been done in 1980, and, as the shift in work took place, information for (internal) program management won out over external information for Congress and the public.

Different Types of Studies

Between 1980 and 1984, the type of work shifted from the more complex evaluations that usually give precise measures of program effects to less complex studies and nontechnical reports. There were fewer of the more time-consuming studies conducted by external evaluators and more of the quicker, less-expensive reports prepared by internal staff.

In our 1988 sample of units, however, there was a greater reliance on external professionals. Unlike earlier years, in which small-scale, quick-turnaround studies were performed by internal professionals, staff shortages in 1988 appeared to have reached a critical level, forcing some units to contract out even small-scale studies. To make matters worse, one of the agency officials suggested that the pool of qualified contractors was itself shrinking.

Between 1980 and 1984, reports increasingly were for internal consumption, produced at the request of program managers and disseminated primarily to them. Evaluations for external consumption—that is, for congressional oversight, for accountability, and for public scrutiny—were limited in number and had usually been mandated by Congress.

Information Loss

These survey findings are consistent with the results of more in-depth GAO studies on key policy issues. These in-depth studies revealed yet another problem: the distortion of findings. For example, in the area of national defense, the quality of program evaluation information on some Defense Department programs is so low that findings are misleading; in other cases, the information is nonexistent. The secretary of Defense and Congress regularly receive data that contain omissions and inaccuracies and assessments that consistently transmit a more favorable presentation of information than is warranted by the facts. This was the case in the tests of the Aegis anti-air system, the Bigeye chemical bomb, and many other weapons systems. In the area of the environment, no one knows whether a number of multibillion dollar environmental programs are effective in achieving planned goals because evaluation information is again misleading and incomplete. Some of the information that is not available concerns the effectiveness of costly efforts to clean up the nation's rivers and streams, hazardous waste volume and capacity, and the health effects of risk-reduction efforts. These programs deal with urgent public health issues and cost billions of dollars; indeed, as with weapons systems, a regular industry has grown up around them. But they have presented little or no systematic evaluation data to show their benefits.

It is important to note that across the federal government there is considerable variation in resources, staff, and evaluation availability and quality. For example, partly as a result of one of our reports, the Center for Educational Statistics in the Department of Education has had a major review of its programs, and important steps have been taken to stabilize leadership, to recruit highly qualified professional staff, and to prioritize and improve the data collection and reporting program. Other agencies also have recruited well-trained evaluators and have made decisions leading to better program evaluation design. Overall, however, the picture is so unsatisfactory that we have called for top-level attention to program evaluation.

Recommendations

We believe that at least four needs may exist, to varying degrees, in many agencies. First, the infrastructure—staff size, staff technical skills, unit placements—has eroded and must be rebuilt. Second, resources must be dedicated to program evaluations and expanded in those agencies where evaluation has disappeared or is not functioning well. Third, priorities must be set by top management so that technically sound information for hearings and reauthorizations will be available. And, fourth, honesty in reporting is a critical priority. Objective data must reach top decision makers, and the review process that helps ensure both technical adequacy and balance must not be allowed to diminish candor.

Need for a Balanced Approach

In general, a better equilibrium should exist, within agencies, among the needs of agency managers for process, formative, and program improvement data; the needs of decision makers in the agencies and in Congress for evaluations that can help formulate new policy; and the needs of Congress and the public for information on program or policy effectiveness. Current evaluation functions, as noted earlier, now produce little of the information on effectiveness that is needed for oversight and for public accountability. This situation requires readjustment. I am not arguing here that internal evaluation is "bad," or external "good." Rather, I am arguing that program evaluation in federal agencies must provide honest information to all of its audiences.

Consequences

What will happen if nothing is done about the decline in executive branch evaluation capabilities? It seems clear that the congressional appetite for evaluative information has not slackened. If the executive agencies do not produce sound, timely program results for oversight and for the public, then the legislative agencies such as GAO, the Congressional Research Service, and the Office of Technology Assessment increasingly may be the voices heard, and agencies could find themselves shut out of important discussions about their own programs. This would be unfortunate in two respects. First, it would surely reduce the amount of information available to improve the management and results of government programs and policies. Second, it would jeopardize the larger balance of power between the executive and legislative branches of government. Over the long term, this would necessarily mean a decrease in the credibility of government vis-à-vis the responsible expenditure of public funds and the pursuit of knowledgeably selected goals.

Recent Results

Having posed these issues for public discussion in November 1988, GAO then briefed Richard Darman, the director of the Office of Management and Budget (OMB), on their ramifications in May 1989. His response was, first, to concur generally with our analysis of the problem and the seriousness of its likely consequences and then to ask us to think about what, precisely, OMB could do to improve the situation. GAO agreed to come up with a plan focusing on long-term institutional change rather than a short-term "fix," assuming tightly constrained staffing and funds.

Proposal to OMB

In November 1989, we sent a discussion paper to Darman on OMB's potential role in governmentwide program evaluation that suggested three goals: an ongoing emphasis on agency program evaluations and use of their findings by OMB staff, the incorporation of evaluation findings into long-term planning, and the performance of evaluations to support presidential initiatives, such as the war on drugs. GAO also proposed that OMB establish a small program evaluation office, with the director having five responsibilities: (1) in-house monitoring, review, and coordination of OMB's program evaluation work; (2) technical oversight of special policy analysis studies for long-term planning; (3) provision of technical assistance for evaluation support for selected presidential initiatives; (4) coordination of program evaluation activities across federal agencies (for example, through guidance on design, analytical, and reporting issues and evaluator recruitment and training); and (5) coordination of program evaluation opportunities between legislative and executive branches (for example, through reviews of mandated and discretionary evaluation studies, and development of an optimum balance between these types of demands on agency resources).

OMB Response

My understanding is that OMB is proceeding to develop such a plan for federal program evaluation under the leadership of Jonathan Breuel. We believe that it is in fact quite possible for OMB to achieve major improvements in program evaluation capabilities both within OMB and across federal agencies with a relatively small expenditure of resources. Indeed, the initiative currently being outlined is small enough in size and useful enough for both short- and long-term purposes to institutionalize flexible support for program evaluation within OMB.

Merely by encouraging and emphasizing the use of strong evaluations, OMB can do a great deal of good. If, in addition, OMB can guarantee the independence of the program evaluation function and ensure its technical competence, the agency should be able to put executive branch program evaluation back on track in the near future, or at the very least to reduce dramatically the serious problems that GAO has identified through agency evaluations over the past decade.

Reference

General Accounting Office. *Program Evaluation Issues.* GAO/OCG-89-8TR. Washington, D.C.: Government Printing Office, 1988.

ELEANOR CHELIMSKY is assistant comptroller general, Program Evaluation and Methodology Division, General Accounting Office.

Evaluation in the U.S. Department of Education declined significantly in the early 1980s. But a search for alternative management strategies and evaluation techniques has allowed the function to survive and prosper.

Meeting the Market for Quality Evaluation in Education

Alan Ginsburg

Evaluation activity at the U.S. Department of Education followed an extreme boom-and-bust cycle. The rise in spending on evaluation of programs during the 1970s and the decline during the first term of the Reagan administration were not much different from the experiences of other agencies. But the subsequent improvement in evaluation resources, which tripled (to $40 million) between the mid-1980s and 1991, and the considerable contribution of evaluations to decision making have been exceptional.

The experience of the Department of Education demonstrates that sustained financial support for evaluations is possible if evaluators produce a high-quality product. However, quality must not be measured against technical soundness alone, although that is important; quality must also be measured against the extent to which evaluations successfully identify and deal with client needs. The achievement of technically sound, user-friendly evaluations is not simple in a world of multiple clients, constraints on time and resources, and limited command over treatment of subjects and controls in education-related studies.

The Department of Education's evaluation experiences demonstrate that effective evaluation management practices can yield high-quality evaluations. This chapter identifies reasons why support for evaluations in the Department of Education waned, considers the strategies that the department used to reinvigorate the evaluation process, and gives examples of

---

The opinions are those of the author and do not necessarily represent those of the U.S. Department of Education. Parts of this chapter are adapted from Ginsburg (1991).

department evaluations that have produced important policy or program-significant findings. The chapter ends with a discussion of ways to improve the quality of evaluations.

The Downturn

Enactment of the Elementary and Secondary Education Act, as part of the War on Poverty during the mid-1960s, represented a significant expansion of the federal role in education. In response, the Department of Education initiated large-scale, nationally representative studies of program effectiveness. This approach was fashioned from the experimental medical model that had been successfully applied to human subjects in evaluations of drug treatments. Outcomes for participants in federal education programs were measured against outcomes for a group of similar students not participating in the program. Because these studies did not hold programs accountable at the local level, eliminate ineffective programs, or guide program improvement, however, the results were disappointing.

Between 1977 and 1981, four independent critiques of the Department of Education's evaluation process (Boruch and Cordray, 1980; Pincus, 1980; Raizen and Rossi, 1981; and General Accounting Office, 1977) raised serious concerns about the policy and operational value of its evaluations. Two types of problems were evident: inadequacies of design and collection of inappropriate information.

Design Inadequacies. The department's evaluation process had three main design problems. First, large-scale longitudinal designs had difficulty isolating program effects. Major education programs are designed to serve all students who are most in need so that it is not feasible to withhold services from an eligible group in order to have a control group for comparison purposes. Statistical procedures employed to adjust for differences among treatment and control populations had not proved robust. Second, evaluations focused only on federally funded services. Even the largest federal programs typically account for only one-fifth of a student's total educational program. The practice of ignoring other educational services seriously flaws model specification. Third, evaluations were one-time efforts that did not take into account the fact that knowledge development is optimally a cumulative process in which evaluation findings build on findings from prior studies. Thus, a single study rarely does more than suggest what works. Follow-on evaluations are needed to corroborate findings under diverse conditions.

Collection of Inappropriate Information. The evaluation process should help clients make better decisions. Policymakers want to improve legislation, and program managers want to boost service quality. Program impact information helps achieve these aims if it is tied to the task of identifying effective practices. By conducting "black box" studies that largely ignored program operations, the department's evaluations did not provide guidance on practices that could produce improvements. Moreover, the large samples needed for developing nationally representative statements about programs would not support the intensive studies needed to link program operations with outcomes.

In addition, the evaluation reports were poorly written and ill-timed. Massive evaluation reports displayed tables of data collected primarily because they were readily reported, rather than because they were useful for improving policies or programs. Information is best organized around program problems and solutions. Furthermore, the completion of studies too late to influence reauthorization added to policymaker frustration with the evaluation process.

Opportunities for Evaluation Renewal

Although the Reagan administration initially attempted to trim the role of the federal government in education, education programs did not disappear. To the contrary, as the 1980s continued, education concerns moved to the forefront of the domestic policy debate, producing a sizeable demand for relevant evaluation information. The challenge was to devise strategies to take advantage of new opportunities. Four strategies were used:

Gaining Top-Level Acceptance. Within a large federal department, such as the Department of Education, authority flows down from the top. Although the central evaluation office, the Planning and Evaluation Service (PES), already had paper responsibility to oversee evaluation activities, evaluation funds were in fact spread around the Department of Education, with little central control. The department could not even list its ongoing evaluation studies, let alone coherently plan them.

Opportunity for reform came about indirectly in 1985 when Secretary of Education William Bennett elected to reorganize the department's research office. PES seized the occasion to ask Secretary Bennett to affirm that PES had responsibility to coordinate evaluation studies for the entire department.

Top management support was essential to initiating turnaround activities. Certain program offices, fearful of losing their autonomy over evaluation funding, resisted PES oversight. These offices reclassified evaluation funds as research or program management studies in order to place them outside the purview of PES. These tactics failed because PES was able to persuade senior department officials to overturn such efforts. Program offices then began taking PES initiatives seriously because they knew PES was supported from the top.

Reaching Out to Clients. The clients for evaluation products are both within and outside the Department of Education. Each group is reached through a different mechanism. Internally, PES and the assistant secretary who oversees each program together develop a multiyear evaluation plan. Now that the program offices realize that the evaluation office will neither step aside as they wanted nor totally absorb their studies as they feared, a cooperative working arrangement has evolved to produce joint ownership of evaluation products.

Outside the department, the two key users of its evaluations are the Congress and the Office of Management and Budget (OMB). Congressional involvement is particularly influential during legislative reauthorization, and congressional support for reauthorization-linked studies has been a major source of growth for the department's evaluation process. The multiyear plan is designed to provide the lead time required to complete studies that conform with legislative reauthorization. The department annually sends Congress its joint multiyear plan, keeps Congress abreast of progress on major studies, and provides briefings on new study findings.

During most of the Reagan years, OMB's top leadership cared little about evaluation, but this attitude has changed. Richard Darman, the current director of OMB, has even gone so far as to suggest that new initiatives should come only from strategies that have been found effective through evaluations of pilots or programs. The OMB annually compares the department's multiyear plan against its own priorities to identify gaps in the department's plan. But OMB does not have veto authority over studies to which Congress has assigned priority. OMB has been particularly influential in promoting performance-based reporting requirements.

Improving Study Design. The best way to prevent failures is to design good studies from the start. Two improvements in methodologies are particularly noteworthy. The first is the adoption of a multiple-study design under which studies of different sizes and purposes are funded simultaneously as an alternative to a single, all-encompassing evaluation. This strategy is particularly critical to the implementation of broad, congressionally mandated studies that are used to prepare for reauthorization of major federal programs. The evaluators review legislative issues specified by Congress, supplemented as necessary to cover all important topics and grouped as appropriate for analysis. One particularly useful framework classifies issues according to their targeting of resources, quality of program services, effectiveness of administration, magnitude of program outcomes, and potential improvement strategies. A matrix of evaluation issues links individual studies with issues addressed.

The second design improvement is the application of rigorous evaluations to the Department of Education's demonstration programs. Most of these demonstrations are run as programs to disburse funds and are not designed to demonstrate anything at all. To overcome local project resistance to rigorous evaluations, requirements for evaluation have been explicitly added as part of the grant competition package, so that prospective grantees buy into evaluations when competing for federal funds. (Prospective grantees who are often willing to accept rigorous evaluations in order to receive funds may resist adding these conditions once their funding is certain.)

Designs that randomly assign potential participants to treatment and control groups also are being introduced. Although random assignment has been applied to several other domestic program areas (Baker-Sucoloski, McKenna, and Boruch, 1991), federal education program administrators have resisted its use, arguing that random assignment unduly intrudes on local authority. In particular, they have expressed the fear that in order to achieve random assignment, evaluators will prevent eligible persons from receiving services. Department of Education program offices have accepted random assignment on the condition that it is limited to situations in which the number of recipients exceeds available services.

Consulting Outside Experts. Effective management of the evaluation process requires an understanding of policy issues, program operations, and evaluation methodologies. The Department of Education recognizes that the knowledge and skills of its staff must be supplemented with those of appropriate outside experts. Moreover, because department employees may have program biases, outside review further serves as a check on objectivity.

The department has two principal strategies for consulting with experts from the field. An evaluation review panel, composed of experts independently nominated by such organizations as the National Academy of Sciences and the American Evaluation Association, meets regularly to review evaluation methodology and to safeguard study objectivity. Additional experts participate on advisory groups for particularly large or difficult studies.

Successful Evaluation Designs

Evaluation of the Department of Education's programs is a challenge. The roughly two hundred legislative authorities range in size of monetary support from the very large (more than $6 billion for compensatory education) to the relatively small (numerous programs are less than $5 million). Not all evaluations have been influential, but enough have yielded payoffs to produce financial support for program assessment.

Successful evaluations have resulted from a variety of methodological designs, including the following:

Descriptive Analyses. These studies assess different aspects of program operations, including funding, services, and administration. Descriptive analyses are particularly useful when actual program operations can be compared against standards for operational efficiency. A descriptive study of new school improvement requirements in the federal compensatory education program concluded that many states had failed to fulfill the intent of this innovative legislation. States were establishing standards that permitted projects to show zero learning gain and still comply with federal school improvement legislation. When these evaluation findings became the focus of congressional testimony, representatives of state-level organizations agreed to establish higher standards of acceptable academic progress. Follow-on evaluations will assess how faithfully the states are keeping to this promise.

The descriptive findings of a long-term study of bilingual education programs (Ramirez, Yuen, and Ramey, 1991) showed that teachers of all types of bilingual programs had adopted a passive approach to language instruction that gave students few opportunities to use language. Research findings on effective language teaching, in contrast, show that proficiency is associated with language usage. The program office is using these findings to change program guidelines and focus technical assistance.

Comparative Cross-Sectional Analyses. Comparative analyses assess projects, at a particular time, against each other or against nonparticipating comparison groups. When comparisons are limited solely to participating projects, they depict a zero-sum process in which some projects are necessarily better than average and others worse. When comparisons include nonparticipating projects, all participating projects may show benefits or deficits.

A comparative analysis was used to fulfill a congressional request to evaluate the financial situation of Howard University, which receives 70 percent of its revenues from federal sources. The distribution of Howard's expenditures was contrasted with the distribution of expenditures by institutions similar to Howard. Although Howard's overall level of spending was similar to that of high-spending research institutions, the study found that Howard actually spent much less, as a fraction of its budget, on research, much more on administration—several times the amounts spent by similar institutions. In response to these findings, Congress has requested that Howard review its spending efficiency.

Student aid defaults annually drains $2 billion from the federal treasury, money that could be used to help more students go to college. To identify aid default patterns among institutions and to control defaults, the Department of Education analyzed more than twenty million records of student aid recipients. It found that some institutions, particularly for-profit schools, accounted for exorbitant amounts of defaults relative to other institutions. The department has used these default rate rankings to identify high default rate institutions and to require them to correct the situation or face dismissal from the federal student aid program.

Expert Judgment Studies. This approach applies the judgment of experts in the field to identify particularly effective programs and practices. Although expert judgment studies are no substitute for carefully designed impact studies that evaluate actual program changes over time, these studies have the advantage of producing results relatively inexpensively and quickly.

The approach is especially useful when expert consensus on best practice is supplemented with corroborative case study evidence on high-performance projects.

The approach has been successfully used in separate evaluations of migrant, gifted, and dropout-prevention programs. All three studies followed the same sequence of reviewing the literature, obtaining expert nominations of effective sites, conducting case studies to validate site performance, and developing guidelines of effective practice based on expert views and site characteristics. The findings from all three studies have been integrated into program operations by establishing model practices to guide program-monitoring efforts and technical assistance. In addition, the dropout-prevention findings were used as the basis for a new rigorous competition to test several treatments that the experts found promising.

Program Impact Analyses. This approach assesses the effects over time of program services on outcomes. These studies differ qualitatively from expert judgment studies in that outcome data, internally generated by the evaluation, provide the raw material for judging program effectiveness. A study of the federal program for educating handicapped students (Wagner, 1989) monitored the post–high school progress of a representative sample of handicapped secondary school students. One year after leaving high school, more than one-third were neither gainfully employed nor attending college. These findings contributed to congressional legislation to strengthen transition services for handicapped persons.

A program in Minnesota offered public high school juniors and seniors the opportunity to enroll free of charge in college courses in postsecondary institutions. Although the evaluation was designed primarily to estimate the direct effects of the program on participants, which were found to be generally favorable, the serendipitous result was an unexpected supply-side effect. Program critics had feared that the program would weaken the public high schools, but in fact the high schools responded to the threatened enrollment loss by substantially expanding their advanced placement offerings. The governor credited these favorable findings with enabling him to expand Minnesota's choice program to permit families to send their children to public schools in other districts.

Simulation Analyses. This method employs mathematical models to analyze alternative policy situations, particularly with respect to federal formula analyses. Simulation analyses were instrumental in the design of a federal formula to distribute compensatory education funds to districts with greatest need. The simulations demonstrated that formulas using the percentage of poor children as an indicator of poverty concentrations helped poor rural communities but failed to help many urban poor. Many major cities are so heterogeneous that a percentage formula does not reflect the large numbers of children at risk for failure who are concentrated in the inner-city areas. Simulation analyses showed that both poor rural and urban areas are reached through a two-factor formula, one factor for large numbers of poor in the cities and a second for high percentages of poor in rural districts. Congress eventually adopted this approach.

Multiple-Study Syntheses. Most large federal programs are complex structures through which government at several levels provides a variety of services to participants with different needs. A single large study is unlikely to represent the optimal design to evaluate all program issues of policy interest. The strategy of funding a number of smaller studies and synthesizing results into a combined program report is often preferred.

The congressionally mandated National Assessment of Vocational Education (NAVE) adopted a multiple-study approach (U.S. Department of Education, 1989). Separate studies explored the targeting of funds to needy students, the relative availability of vocational education services for low-income and other communities, the quality of vocational services, and the reporting of program performance data. Chairman Augustus Hawkins of the House Education and Labor Committee publicly credited the NAVE findings as being influential in the production of new legislation that directed additional federal vocational funds to low-income areas, integrated vocational with academic services, and required state performance standards.

Management Strategies to Continue to Improve the Evaluation Process

Product improvement must be a continuing process that builds on past gains and responds to changing conditions. Within education, three improvement areas are particularly noteworthy:

Applying Total Quality Management (TQM). The ability to produce high-quality studies that satisfy evaluation clients is the key to the turnaround in the Department of Education's evaluation process. The TQM model is designed to produce high-quality products with users in mind. This approach, successfully applied in the private sector, is now being applied to public service provision.

Principles of TQM that emerged from the department's experience managing the process are as follows:

Meeting Client Needs. The evaluator has multiple clients: policymakers in the legislative and executive branches, federal program managers, local operations personnel, and program recipients. Although program recipients are the ultimate clients for services, evaluators should seek to expand their markets to new users of evaluation findings. Evaluations need to have meaning for the lawmakers in the Congress and the educators in the classrooms. In education evaluation, local evaluators remain a relatively untapped, yet potentially valuable market. This TQM principle can also improve evaluations by enabling the evaluator to balance different user requirements.

Preventing Evaluation Problems from Occurring Rather than Fixing Them After They Have Occurred. Prevention of problems is considerably cheaper than their correction after they have occurred. The ability to foresee the kinds of evaluations that are likely to be worthwhile, and to effectively control the evaluation process, depends on considerable front-end investment (for example, through the multiyear planning process).

Sharing Decision Making. Evaluators treasure their independence, but going it alone has been costly. Isolation within the Department of Education protected evaluators from unwarranted political pressure, but isolation also produced studies that lacked relevance, timeliness, and a sense of ownership by the administrators whose programs were under review. Rather than ignore frontline program staff who are particularly knowledgeable about program concerns, evaluators should seek to ensure objectivity through other means, including independent expert reviews.

Continually Reassessing and Improving the Evaluation Process. While evaluators evaluate others, there is always the question of who is to evaluate the evaluators. The day of reckoning always comes, as it eventually did during the 1980s, when policymakers curtail spending for evaluation studies that they deem unworthy of the costs. The challenge for the evaluator is to assess accomplishments accurately and continually to prevent costly mistakes and to identify new opportunities for improvement.

Developing Performance-Based Management Information Systems (MISs). MISs are not new management tools, but perhaps because of reliance on self-reported information, evaluators have made the mistake of not viewing MISs as important potential sources of information. While MISs cannot produce data of the quality of a rigorous evaluation, they can fill other requirements. Data collection is universal and relatively efficient when it can be used by the projects as well as the federal policymaker. The availability of universal information means that individual projects can be held accountable for performance.

However, MISs could be significantly improved by focusing on the collection of performance data instead of the general descriptive data usually compiled. Performance indicators yield judgments about the effectiveness of a program or its components. For example, performance indicators may reveal a program's effectiveness in reaching eligible populations, in providing services of sufficient intensity or duration to make a difference, or in affecting the outcomes of participants measured against learning objectives.

Evaluating Innovative Treatments. Although the Department of Education has tightened its evaluation requirements for program demonstrations, educational breakthroughs will remain insignificant so long as demonstration projects fail to represent truly innovative practices. Indeed, the delivery of education services has changed little during the twentieth century, and the department's demonstrations rarely support fundamental change.

In contrast, nonprofit foundations devote considerable resources to identifying promising new approaches that explicitly test relatively radical ideas in a number of places. Many of the ideas represent significant risk taking in the sense that they radically depart from the present situation. Few foundation projects, however, are subject to rigorous evaluation. Federal demonstration programs that link significant new ideas to rigorous evaluation can provide a major source of new knowledge for education improvement.

References

Baker-Sucoloski, T., McKenna, L., and Boruch, B. F. *Abstracts of Randomized Experiments for Planning, Developing, and Evaluating Domestic Programs and Projects.* Report No. P-531. Philadelphia: Graduate School of Education, University of Pennsylvania, 1991.

Boruch, R. F., and Cordray, D. *An Appraisal of Educational Program Evaluations: Federal, State, and Local Agencies.* Contract #300-79-0467. Washington, D.C.: Government Printing Office, 1980.

General Accounting Office. *Problems and Needed Improvements in Evaluating Office of Education Programs.* Report No. GAO/HRD 76-165. Washington, D.C.: Government Printing Office, 1977.

Ginsburg, A. "Fulfilling the Promise of Program Evaluation." *The Bureaucrat,* Fall 1991, pp. 49–52.

Pincus, J. (ed.). *Education Evaluation in the Public Policy Setting.* Santa Monica, Calif.: Rand Corporation, 1980.

Raizen, S., and Rossi, P. *Program Evaluation: When? How? To What Ends?* Washington, D.C.: National Academy of Sciences, 1981.

Ramirez, J., Yuen, S., and Ramey, D. *Longitudinal Study of Structured Immersion Strategy: Early Exit and Late Exit Transitional Bilingual Programs for Language Minority Children.* San Mateo, Calif.: Aguirre International, 1991.

U.S. Department of Education. *National Assessment of Vocational Education (NAVE).* Final Report. Washington, D.C.: Government Printing Office, 1989.

Wagner, M. *The Transition Experiences of Youth with Disabilities: A Report from the National Longitudinal Transition Study.* Washington, D.C.: U.S. Department of Education, 1989.

ALAN GINSBURG is director of the Planning and Evaluation Service at the U.S. Department of Education.

In response to repeated budget and staffing reductions, the Office of Program Analysis and Evaluation developed a series of innovative approaches to lower the cost and increase the utility of its evaluation work. But, ultimately, the effort was unsuccessful, and the office was reorganized into a policy coordination office.

Evaluation in the Department of Housing and Urban Development

David B. Rymph

The story of evaluation in the U.S. Department of Housing and Urban Development (HUD) between 1980 and 1988 is one of adjustment to straitened circumstances and, ultimately, of dissolution of the function. Early in 1981, the new administration reduced the budgets and staffing for evaluation and research by two-thirds. In this chapter, I begin by depicting HUD's evaluation system in 1980. I then describe the 1981 budget cuts and lay out some of the survival strategies adopted by two of HUD's largest evaluation units. Finally, I depict the state of HUD's evaluation system at the beginning of 1989.

Evaluation in HUD, 1980

In fall 1980, program evaluation existed at three levels of the department. Under the secretary, eight assistant secretaries managed HUD, each in charge of either an administrative area or a major program. Regional directors managed HUD's field operations from ten locations around the country. Each of these top managers had a direct reporting line to the secretary of the department.

The highest-level unit of the department involved in evaluation resided within the Office of the Assistant Secretary for Policy Development and

---

The opinions expressed in this chapter are those of the author and do not necessarily represent those of the U.S. Department of Housing and Urban Development. This chapter is reprinted, with permission, with minor revisions from *Evaluation Practice,* 1989, *10* (2), 30–39.

Research (PD&R). PD&R was the largest and most active research and evaluation unit in HUD, and it served as HUD's in-house think tank. It also provided overall coordination to the department's program evaluation activities. Both the authority and the budget for most of HUD's program evaluation efforts resided in PD&R.

Three evaluation units served assistant secretaries in charge of major programs: Community Planning and Development (CPD), Housing, and Fair Housing and Equal Opportunity. The largest of these units was the Office of Evaluation under the assistant secretary for CPD. This chapter focuses on two units, PD&R and OE. These two offices were the preeminent evaluation units in HUD in 1980. They continue to be the major contributors to HUD's overall evaluation capacity today.

In the mid-1970s, evaluation in HUD had a relatively formal structure. PD&R served as the overall coordinator of evaluation in the department. Ideally, agreed-on terms structured the relationship between PD&R and all other evaluation offices (excluding the Office of the Inspector General). Under these terms, other units would propose studies to PD&R, which then set the research and evaluation agenda for the department. PD&R held final authority for the use of funds from its program evaluation budget, $6.1 million in 1980. It also held final review authority over all study proposals that wished to draw on that budget. This system was designed to systematize the relationships between PD&R and other evaluation units. PD&R had to be able to ensure the quality and integrity of evaluations done throughout HUD.

HUD was actively evaluating its programs in the late 1970s, and the resources devoted to evaluation activities reflected this activity. PD&R in 1980 had a budget of $45 million and a staff of 205. It had an Evaluation Division specifically to do long-term evaluation studies and a Special Studies Division to focus on short-term projects. Much of the evaluation budget in PD&R went to the support of long-term impact studies. These were expensive and large-scale projects. They often involved a mix of in-house government staff, university-based researchers, and private consulting firms.

At the second level of evaluation, HUD's program offices were also active. The Office of CPD was responsible for managing HUD's major urban programs. To support these programs in 1980, CPD's Office of Evaluation (OE) had twenty-five permanent staff members. In addition, there was a large complement of temporary staff made up of academics on temporary (six months to a year) assignment to CPD, graduate students, and data coders. At one time in 1980, the total number of OE staff reached sixty. To support its program evaluation activities, OE had an informal annual draw of $1 million on PD&R's program evaluation budget. Another measure of its activity was a budget line of $241,000 in 1980 for special contract support.

OE concentrated its efforts in two areas. First, it focused on process evaluations that supported the management of CPD's programs. Its methodology consisted primarily of case studies and survey research, usually in a short time frame of three to nine months. Second, it produced the annual reports to Congress on CPD's five major programs.

The structure of evaluation in 1980 can be summarized this way. At each level of the organization, there were at least two options available to managers wanting evaluation support. First, the secretary of HUD, each assistant secretary, and seven of the ten regional administrators had control of an evaluation unit. At each level, this evaluation unit was independent of the program offices. This independence enabled each unit to maintain a measure of objectivity that might not have been there had the unit been attached directly to a major program. The second option was that managers at each of these levels could ask for funds or staff resources from an external evaluation unit, PD&R. PD&R was, in effect, the secretary's evaluation unit, but even the secretary had a quasi-external authority in the Office of the Inspector General.

1981: A Year of Change

The presidential election in fall 1980 ushered in a period of rapid change for HUD's evaluation system. The first one hundred days of the new administration brought immediate budget cuts. Research efforts were sharply scaled back. With the new president's first budget, the PD&R budget was cut from approximately $45 million to $37 million, a drop of 18 percent. By 1983, it had been reduced to $18 million, down 60 percent from its 1980 level. Of that $18 million, $11 million was to be transferred each year, according to practice dating back to the mid-1970s, to the Bureau of the Census to pay for the collection of housing data. The number of permanent, full-time staff dropped from 205 in 1980 to 168 by 1983. From that time, PD&R's budget remained relatively constant while staff levels continued to drop (see Table 7.1), except that beginning in 1988 both figures turned slightly upward.

OE, under the assistant secretary for CPD, also experienced losses of support. While full-time permanent staff were cut from twenty-five in 1980 to twenty-three in 1981, the number reached a low of eighteen in 1984. A big loss in 1981 was the almost immediate departure of all the temporary staff, including ten university professors on leave to work with OE. These highly trained and experienced researchers had been a major part of the office's evaluation capacity. Financial research support also dropped in 1981. Special contract support dropped from $241,000 to $200,000 (see Table 7.2).

Strategies for Survival

It was a much changed climate of very limited resources for evaluation in 1981. PD&R and OE worked to develop strategies that would enable them

Table 7.1. Budget and Staff Levels in the Office of Policy Development and Research, 1980-1987

Year	*Budget*	*Staff*
1980	$44,650,000	205
1981	$37,208,000	193
1982	$21,273,000	168
1983	$18,000,000	168
1984	$19,200,000	145
1985	$16,900,000	143
1986	$16,173,000	143
1987	$17,000,000	135

Table 7.2. Staff and Research Support in the Office of Evaluation/Office of Program Analysis and Evaluation, 1980-1988

Year	*Full-Time Permanent Staff*	*University Researchers*	*Special Contract Support*	*Studies*	*Policy Development and Research*
1980	25	10	$241,000	0	$1,000,000
1981	23	0	$200,000	0	0
1982	19	0	$200,000	$100,000	0
1983	20	0	$200,000	$75,000	0
1984	18	0	$200,000	0	0
1985	21	0	$200,000	0	0
1986	20	0	$200,000	0	0
1987	23	0	$150,000	0	0
1988	26	0	$200,000	0	0

to survive. In general, these strategies sought to reorganize, reduce the scale of activity, seek efficiencies in operation, and develop new techniques in evaluation.

Reorganization. Both PD&R and OE sought to maintain some leverage in the department by redefining their functions and reorganizing to better serve the needs of the new administration. Even before the Reagan years, PD&R was moving away from a structure that segmented research evaluation and policy development. By July 1982, PD&R had dissolved its Evaluation Division and distributed that division's functions across the offices within PD&R. One reason given for this change was that because much of the work in other divisions was also evaluation, no need existed for a separate unit.

In 1982, at the direction of the assistant secretary, OE reorganized and took on a new title, the Office of Program Analysis and Evaluation (OPAE). The addition of "program analysis" to the title was an effort to tie the office to a broader agenda than evaluation. This change was part of an emerging strategy to give the office a larger role in CPD, to move it beyond its identification as a research unit without influence in management decision making. Divisions within the office were realigned. New division titles and functions appeared. Where before the division titles had reflected methodological specialties, the new titles were topical and linked each division to specific CPD programs.

Reductions in Scale of Activity. Major cuts in overall effort took place in both offices due to reduced resources. In addition to dissolving the Evaluation Division, PD&R dropped the program evaluation budget line, which meant a $1 million loss to OPAE. PD&R narrowed the range of research and evaluation topics that it would support. Whole areas of research were eliminated or transferred to other departments. For example, PD&R completely dropped funding for research in energy conservation and solar technology, a cut of $2.3 million. Each year, as the administration or Congress cut its budget, PD&R produced fewer reports. In 1980, PD&R had sponsored 347 reports in cooperation with other offices and organizations. In 1981, the total sponsored reports dropped to 183.

One of the most important responses by PD&R to the reduction in resources resulted from the decline in funds for contract research. PD&R shifted away from evaluation requiring large-scale primary data collection. More emphasis was placed on policy analysis based on existing research and data, which in turn led to greater reliance on in-house staff. Analyses began to take the form of policy memoranda rather than formal reports. The time frame for production of reports began to decrease.

Before the cuts, OPAE had divided its resources as follows: annual reports to Congress, 50 percent; short-term analysis (one day to three months), 25 percent; long-term contract research (three to nine months), 25 percent. With the loss of temporary research support, OPAE focused two-thirds of its resources on the production of CPD's annual reports to Congress. OPAE dropped all long-term research. Any resources remaining after production of the annual reports went to support short-term analysis and evaluation.

Efficiencies of Operation. One approach designed to increase the overall efficiency of the department was to reemphasize PD&R's role as coordinator and overseer of the department's evaluation system. The intent of this policy was to eliminate overlap and duplication among the various departmental evaluation units. With fewer resources, the goal was to use what was left more wisely. A memo from the secretary was sent to executive staff in April 1981. Specifically, the memo laid out these guidelines: (1) All research for HUD is to be done by PD&R. (2) Demonstrations of new or proposed programs are to be designed by PD&R. It has the authority to determine who operates the demonstrations. (3) PD&R has "preeminent responsibility for all program evaluation," which includes impact, feasibility, and early assessment evaluations. (4) Performance (operations) evaluations are the responsibility of the assistant secretaries and the regional administrators. This area of evaluation focuses on management issues of staff productivity, compliance with regulations, and monitoring.

OPAE also sought greater efficiency in operation. A major cost saving was found in the annual reports to Congress. OPAE combined what were then five separate reports into one combined annual report to Congress. OPAE estimated that the cost savings realized by the combined annual report amounted to approximately $200,000. With the loss of support for long-term studies, the time frame for OPAE studies became shorter, but the office did more of them. Other savings were made by restructuring contract support. Where before contractors had been used for analysis, they were now limited to data collection and coding.

New Techniques in Evaluation. Before 1981, OPAE mainly carried out discrete studies and had little involvement in the day-to-day operations of the Office of CPD. Beginning in 1981, OPAE began to focus on short-term management information issues. Over time, OPAE evolved to become the assistant secretary's policy and program analysis support staff, performing a range of functions much broader than just evaluation.

Finding itself in an environment that put little trust in traditional approaches to evaluation, OPAE began a search for useful tasks that it could fulfill for the assistant secretary. It sought functions that, while not traditionally identified with evaluation, were built on the skills of the profession. What developed was a progressive series of innovative uses of analytical and evaluation techniques, beginning with basic and simple services to the assistant secretary and moving to more complex research and analytical tasks.

OPAE began its efforts to prove useful by producing two- to three-page briefing papers on topics of immediate interest to the assistant secretary. These papers could serve any number of purposes—for example, the provision of data on issues that arose in the newspapers or the assembling of background information on new program proposals. The new assistant secretary did not invite these papers; OPAE produced them as demonstrations of initiative, analytical ability, and relevance. The briefing papers came to have a receptive audience among the political appointees.

Building on the success of the briefing papers, the office developed next a series of analytical tracking charts. Through use of relatively basic graphic techniques, the charts mapped the important milestones of new management initiatives. In addition to tracking progress, the charts identified future stages of the initiatives that would require or could benefit from the production of analytical and evaluation information. The strategy was to get the office, by way of the information it could produce, into the stream of decision making. Within CPD, this was a controversial move because OPAE had never before taken such an active part in the management of programs and policies. Some resistance was encountered from other offices in CPD, but the assistant secretary found the simple graphics to be useful.

Moving to increase further its utility to the new management of CPD, OPAE undertook a series of local government field surveys. In these surveys, OPAE gathered the views of the nation's mayors on what they thought of CPD's performance. The methodology consisted of semistructured interviews, conducted face to face by OPAE staff, covering one region of the country in each survey.

When the surveys first began, some program offices expressed concern that they might be biased because only one constituent group was being polled, and a highly political one at that. Aware of these concerns, OPAE carefully maintained confidentiality on all information. While the assistant secretary might want to know, for political purposes, which mayor said what, OPAE aggregated data and disguised responses so that identities were protected. As the results of the surveys were made known, it became apparent that the mayors were providing very useful information. A gradual accommodation by the program offices occurred, and they came to value the data gathered by the surveys. The result proved to be a useful overview of what one of HUD's most important client groups thought of its programs.

The preceding techniques share an important strategic characteristic that helped ensure their success: Each technique was introduced piecemeal. Instead of trying to sell evaluation through proposals for formal studies, the introduction of each technique began with a single, limited example of its application. If it failed, few resources had been expended, and the office was in a position to recover its losses and try another approach. On the other hand, the success of an initial small-scale trial paved the way for more and larger applications of evaluation techniques.

With those initial successes, the office had established a position in CPD from which it could launch a large-scale study. OPAE proposed an anticipatory evaluation of new legislation for CPD's largest project, the Community Development Block Grant Program. Several major legislative changes were made to the Block Grant Program in 1981. By gathering information during the first thirty days of the new regulations, the anticipatory evaluation sought to assess the importance and scope of program trends coincident with the implementation of the new initiatives. OPAE planned for its anticipatory evaluations to be a part of program development, providing information to program managers and increasing their ability to identify and address issues and problems in new CPD programs as they arose.

That OPAE was regaining the confidence of CPD's leadership was confirmed when the assistant secretary decided to use OPAE to evaluate a major management initiative. OPAE was asked to conduct an evaluation assessment of CPD's entire management system and was given three weeks in which to complete it. Given the short time frame, OPAE developed a tiered brainstorming technique that could quickly gather a lot of information from several levels of the CPD hierarchy.

The evaluation assessment began with nonsupervisory professional staff, brainstorming a few key questions on CPD planning. Their ideas were collated and given to the next higher level, the division directors, to review. They could not change the comments but could add to them in their own brainstorming sessions. At the highest level, office directors could add their views but not change the comments from those lower in the hierarchy. Finally, OPAE organized all the comments and added an analysis of existing departmental documents. The office presented this summary of findings to the assistant secretary within the deadline, and the summary served as the basis for redesigning the management planning process.

Summary of Strategies for Survival. PD&R and OPAE followed some of the same basic survival strategies: reorganization, more efficient operation, and reduction in scale of operation. That they also had divergent strategies was a function of whom they served and the resources available. PD&R worked for the secretary of HUD and took a broad, departmentwide view of its role. It was also taking some very large budget cuts. The combination of its position and resource level led it to place increasing emphasis on policy analysis and less on basic research.

OPAE served the assistant secretary of CDP. After initial rejection, OPAE moved through a progressive series of evaluation activities into a position of acceptance and influence. OPAE followed a strategy of starting with basic, simple products and progressively increasing the scope of activity and its utility. While maintaining its base as an evaluation unit, OPAE increasingly became the assistant secretary's analytical support staff on a range of management and program issues.

Evaluation in HUD, 1988

In 1988, evaluation in HUD stood at a level far below that of 1980. PD&R's annual budget was still $18 million, nearly $2 million above the lowest point reached in 1986. In 1987, its permanent full-time staff was at its lowest point, 135. The remaining staff consisted primarily of economists or other social scientists with a heavy quantitative background. (The assistant secretaries have been political scientists.)

PD&R was a very different organization in 1988 from what it was in 1980. There was less basic research, less technical assistance, fewer unsolicited research and demonstration proposals being funded, and a reduced emphasis on building technology research. There was a major shift within PD&R in the relative emphasis between in-house and contract work during the 1980s. A much larger percentage of the staff is capable of doing in-house research and are doing it.

OPAE's permanent staff rebounded from its low of eighteen in 1984 to twenty-six in 1988. The model professional category is political science, but a wide range of disciplines is represented, including anthropology, law, planning, public administration, and sociology. OPAE continues to emphasize short-term, quick turnaround, management-oriented evaluations. It mainly studies operational and policy issues of immediate interest to the assistant secretary and his program offices. OPAE increasingly paid attention to the task of developing techniques for improving communication between HUD in Washington, D.C., and its national network of field offices.

Future of Evaluation in HUD

Beginning with the change of administrations in 1989, PD&R's budget began to increase, and Congress made specific staffing allocations for an evaluation function. In 1991, PD&R reestablished a specific division with responsibility for evaluation. The division is beginning to map out an evaluation plan. During the same period of time, OPAE was reorganized as a policy coordination unit. The mission of the new unit was defined as coordinating the implementation of policy. Evaluation and analytical activities contributing to the development or evaluation of policy were specifically excluded from its functions. Its major purpose was defined as ensuring the implementation of policy as designed.

The federal deficit will probably continue to prevent or severely limit any growth of evaluation in HUD. The department will continue to operate on a very lean budget. Policymakers for HUD will have to make tough choices. The program issues that have been the main foci of the department's programs—housing, public infrastructure, economic development—will continue well beyond the end of this century.

Of course, the future may bring no growth or even a decline in support for evaluation. PD&R and OPAE survived the drastic cuts in the early years of the Reagan administration. While surviving, they learned that evaluation is not always accepted as an essential component of bureaucracy. The lesson of the 1980s for evaluators in federal service is that they are always subject to test. They must prove to each new set of political appointees that evaluation can serve their political interests while continuing to serve the public good.

DAVID B. RYMPH is director, Program Analysis and Evaluation Division, ACTION, in Washington, D.C.

Using rapid, in-house evaluation, the inspectors general have helped top decision makers improve program efficiency, effectiveness, and integrity at many federal departments.

The Inspectors General

Michael F. Mangano

One of the most interesting—and controversial—developments in program evaluation today is the growing role of the federal Offices of Inspectors General (OIGs). These "junkyard dogs," widely misperceived as caring only about fiscal audits and criminal investigations, have been slowly but surely developing a third capability: program inspections or, simply, inspections. While the specifics of these inspections vary from one OIG to another, different inspections have improved the quality of services, made services more efficient, identified vulnerabilities to fraud, and saved money. In other words, the best inspection resembles that elusive goal—an effective evaluation study.

However, most of us know very little, if anything, about these OIG evaluators. Who are these people? Do they really do "evaluation" as we know it? How do they do their evaluations? How well? And, perhaps most important, what does their work mean for more traditional evaluations and evaluators? In other words, are OIG inspections a healthy direction for growth or an ominous sign for the future?

At least one person answers "ominous sign." Kathryn E. Newcomer (1989, p. 60), in listing ways to kill evaluation, says that one technique is to "urge upper management to transfer all evaluation responsibilities to the Inspector General (IG) in their agency. Ferreting out fraud and abuse is much more appealing to politicians than analyzing program operations and

---

The opinions expressed in this chapter are those of the author and do not necessarily represent or reflect the positions of the Offices of Inspectors General. This chapter is reprinted, with permission, with minor revisions from *The Bureaucrat,* 1990, *19* (4), 13–15.

impact. Once evaluation has been transferred to the IG's office then one can simply let the IG staff finish off the job. The IG can convince any political appointee that auditing really is evaluation, and evaluation really is auditing, and auditing is actually auditing, and evaluation is actually nothing more to speak of." Either Newcomer is prescient or someone was paying close attention, because the Department of Justice took her advice and moved all its evaluation units (save that of the FBI) to its OIG. Is this a serious mistake or a brilliant innovation? Or is the truth somewhere in between?

A Short History of OIG Evaluations

When OIGs first began operating, most had two functions: (1) accountants and other financial management experts to audit agency expenditures and (2) law enforcement experts to investigate criminal, civil, and administrative wrongdoing. But two factors were uniting to change this arrangement.

First, decision makers at all levels and in all branches of government were becoming disenchanted with "traditional" program evaluation. While there were exceptions, evaluations generally were contracted out to consulting firms or universities, required rigorous methodology, were quite expensive, produced thick, scholarly reports, and took an average of two years to complete. Perhaps partly because of this dissatisfaction, the General Accounting Office (GAO) found in 1988 that the agencies examined in its study had cut their evaluation staffs in half since 1980 (GAO, 1988).

Second, when the Reagan administration took office in 1981, the budget became a focal point for all discussions, and decision makers increasingly wanted to know the budget implications on all issues. Unfortunately, traditional evaluators have historically had little information to contribute to these "dollar decisions." But others, such as OIG auditors, have had relevant data at their disposal. As a result, inspectors general (IGs) were included in these decisions and began to be seen as key players in programmatic decisions.

It was a short step from this OIG role to a role of conducting evaluations, since the OIG missions are to (1) promote the economy, efficiency, and effectiveness of federal operations and (2) prevent and detect fraud, waste, and mismanagement. The ability to increase efficiency and effectiveness, or to decrease waste and mismanagement, requires the capacity to assess these characteristics in the first place.

Program Inspections Today

The IGs saw, though, that audits and investigations alone could not provide this assessment capacity, so many of them created a third unit for inspections. Eight of the twenty-four presidentially appointed IGs (Commerce, Defense, Energy, General Services Administration [GSA], Health and Human Services [HHS], Justice, State, and United States Information Agency [USIA]) presently operate inspections functions, and these eight IGs have oversight responsibility for approximately 75 percent of all federal expenditures.

In addition, four more IGs (Education, Labor, Office of Personnel Management, and Veterans Administration) operate functions similar to inspections, and three (Railroad Retirement Board, Small Business Administration, and Transportation) intend to develop inspections functions. In all, over half of these twenty-four IGs either currently operate inspectionslike functions or they will in the near future.

Table 8.1 presents partial data from a 1989 survey (Moran, 1989) by the President's Council on Integrity and Efficiency (PCIE). This survey gathered the information for the first comprehensive look at OIG inspections activities. Six of the eight IGs with active inspections functions have established distinct units for this activity, with two IGs lodging this activity inside other offices. From an organizational perspective, the establishment of a distinct identity for the inspections function may suggest that IGs view this activity as not only important to the OIG mission but also as likely to continue for the foreseeable future.

Regarding the scope of inspections, OIG staff conduct four, quite different types of studies: (1) snapshot studies (for example, What does the organization or program look like in actual operation?), (2) compliance reviews (for example, Is the organization or program doing what it is required to do?), (3) efficiency and effectiveness studies (for example, How well and at what cost is the organization or program doing what is required?), and (4) policy analysis studies (for example, Should the organization's or program's legislation, regulations, or policies be changed?). In practice, these types of studies are manifest as either (1) systemic looks at broadly defined issues or programs, or (2) more targeted looks at narrowly focused policies, issues, or organizations. To an outside observer, systemic inspections look very much like program evaluations, while targeted inspections more closely resemble audits. Table 8.1 lists, first, the one OIG (HHS) that conducts mostly systemic inspections (that is, inspections most like evaluations), then the three OIGs (Defense, USIA, and State) that conduct a mix of both systemic and targeted studies, then the remaining OIGs (Commerce, Energy, and GSA) that conduct mostly targeted inspections (that is, inspections most like audits).

The sizes of the inspections units vary from 12 professionals (Commerce) to 170 (Defense). It is not surprising that OIGs also differ in the types of staff placed in these units, with a wide variety of job classifications appearing across agencies. Table 8.1 lists some of these staff backgrounds, which appear to correlate with staff conduct of systemic versus targeted studies. Those OIGs that conduct mostly systemic studies (or a mix of both systemic and targeted studies) rely heavily on program analysts, manage-

Table 8.1. Characteristics of OIG Inspections Units

Agency	*Location Within OIG*	*Scope of Most Inspections*	*Backgrounds of Most Staff*
Health and Human Services	Distinct unit	Systemic	Program analysts
Defense	Distinct unit	Systemic/Targeted	Program analysts
United States Information Agency	Distinct unit	Systemic/Targeted	Management analysts and foreign service auditors
State	Investigations/ Security oversight officers	Systemic/Targeted	Program generalists and foreign service
Commerce	Distinct unit	Targeted	Accountants, auditors, and economists
Energy	Distinct unit	Targeted	General investigators and general engineers
General Services Administration	Audit	Targeted	Auditors
Justice[a]			

[a] A distinct inspections unit is currently being established.

Source: Based on Moran, 1989.

ment analysts, or program generalists. In contrast, OIGs that conduct mostly targeted studies rely heavily on auditors and other technical experts. This split makes sense given the different orientations of these different staffs, and it also suggests that the PCIE's best predictor of an OIG's approach to inspections might be the types of staff placed in that unit.

For all types of inspections and for all staff, the issue of inspections standards is critical. In the past, many OIG inspectors have adhered to the government auditing standards (GAO's [1989] famous "Yellow Book"), both because many inspectors were originally trained as auditors and because auditors and inspectors are often in close proximity to each other in OIG offices. Most inspectors also use the general standards that PCIE (1986) developed to govern all OIG work.

Recently, however, explicit standards have been developed specifically for OIG inspections. The HHS OIG began this process by developing its own inspections standards in 1986, basing them partially on the two sets of standards endorsed by the American Evaluation Association (OIG, 1986).

In 1990, a PCIE committee advanced this work by drafting a set of standards applicable to all inspections activities in all OIGs (PCIE, 1990). OIG inspectors are convinced that by having their own standards, they are better able to ensure the quality of their work.

Traits Common to Most Inspections

While OIG inspections differ across agencies, they also possess several traits in common, including the following:

Short Time Frames. Perhaps the most common theme of inspections is the emphasis on timeliness. Most studies, whether systemic or targeted, are completed within two to six months. Inspectors are convinced that this speed helps to stimulate and maintain interest among decision makers.

Use of In-House Staff. Almost all inspections activities are conducted by full-time OIG employees, with almost no contracting with private individuals or firms. Inspectors believe that this approach speeds the studies, helps to protect confidentiality, and provides better and more consistent communications.

Diverse Methodologies. There is no single inspections method that is applied in all, or even most, studies. Depending on the topic, inspectors gather information via computerized extraction of data from existing data bases, document reviews, record reviews, personal discussions, mailed surveys (with full review and approval by the Office of Management and Budget), observations of various sorts (including unobtrusive measures), special tests or demonstrations, and/or case studies.

Independent Publication of Findings. Evaluators, especially internal evaluators working inside an agency, sometimes find it difficult to report findings that potentially embarrass or contradict an administration's position. IGs, on the other hand, enjoy the luxury of being required to send reports directly to Congress every six months and to bypass their agencies' respective chains of command when they do so.

Strong Promotion of Findings and Recommendations. Because of the OIG mission, inspectors are expected to promote their findings and recommendations aggressively. Sonnichsen (1988, p. 142) calls this aggressive salesmanship "advocacy evaluation," and OIG inspectors use both short written reports and personal briefings to "champion" their information.

Apparent Strengths of OIG Inspections

Advocates of inspections see at least four strengths in this new approach to evaluation. First, the unique organizational location of an OIG allows evaluators to be both "inside" yet "outside" their agency at the same time. There have been many discussions in the evaluation literature about which location is better for evaluators, and the OIGs represent an interesting variation that seems to have it both ways. Second, this organizational location provides insulation from many of the pressures that other evaluators have to face. The ability to publish independently and promote findings and recommendations was mentioned above. Third, the OIG also brings a measure of financial security that is not present in many other evaluation units. In a time of increasingly scarce federal dollars, OIGs are still considered one of the "fair-haired" children of the administration, and their inspectors are still relatively well funded. Fourth, OIG evaluators have the opportunity to become highly visible. It is not at all unusual for an IG to testify before Congress on the results of an inspection, or for inspection results to appear on the front pages of major newspapers, on network news programs, in newsmagazines, or on radio programs. As a result of this exposure, OIG inspections may well serve to define, for many important audiences, just exactly what an "evaluation" is.

Concerns About OIG Inspections

Not everyone, however, is an advocate for OIG inspections, and a number of questions have been raised about their quality and appropriateness. These questions have not yet been answered, but discussion about them helps to advance the field.

A first set of questions concerns the quality of the inspections themselves: Regarding the selection of topics to study, does the OIG's natural concern with fiscal issues inevitably bias inspectors toward selecting large-budget issues to study? Are inspections too reactive; that is, should they help to shape the agenda of questions asked in addition to responding to decision makers' questions? Do inspections look too closely at government operations and not closely enough at total programs?

Regarding the conduct of inspections, do all inspectors have the skills required for this work? Are the chosen methods appropriate, or does an undue emphasis on timeliness preclude use of more appropriate, but slower, methods? What signals do unannounced visits (as in Commerce) send to program managers? How can quality control be ensured—are the standards sufficient, or should someone be watching the watchdog?

A second set of questions raises even more difficult issues about the proper role of OIG inspections. What should be the overall "portfolio" of evaluative activities conducted in an executive branch agency? How can inspections fit into that mix? How should OIG inspectors relate to OIG auditors, to evaluators in the more traditional evaluation offices, and to the GAO? Finally, and perhaps most important, as inspections become even more successful, will agency decision makers be reluctant to fund other types of evaluations that are also needed?

Conclusion

These are difficult questions, but they need to be addressed. One would have to be very naive to believe that the OIGs' successes at the federal level will not affect evaluations at state and local levels. If inspections continue to gain attention, more state and local legislators will attempt to create similar functions in their own agencies. Needless to say, these state and local functions could affect evaluations at those levels as much as OIGs are affecting evaluations at the national level.

References

General Accounting Office. *Program Evaluation Issues.* Washington, D.C.: Government Printing Office, 1988.

General Accounting Office. *Government Auditing Standards.* Washington, D.C.: Government Printing Office, 1989.

Moran, W. *Draft PCIE Inspection Standards.* Washington, D.C.: Office of Inspector General, U.S. Department of Health and Human Services, 1989.

Newcomer, K. E. "Ten Ways to Kill Program Evaluation." *Bureaucrat,* Fall 1989, 59–60.

Office of Inspector General. *Standards for Program Inspections.* U.S. Department of Health and Human Services. Washington, D.C.: Government Printing Office, 1986.

President's Council on Integrity and Efficiency. *Quality Standards for Federal Offices of Inspector General.* Washington, D.C.: Government Printing Office, 1986.

President's Council on Integrity and Efficiency. *Interim Standards for Inspections.* Washington, D.C.: Government Printing Office, 1990.

Sonnichsen, R. C. "Advocacy Evaluation: A Model for Internal Evaluation Offices." *Evaluation and Program Planning,* 1988, *11,* 141–148.

MICHAEL F. MANGANO *is deputy inspector general, Office of Evaluation and Inspections, Office of the Inspector General, U.S. Department of Health and Human Services.*

In the early 1980s, the Office of Management and Budget withdrew its support for program evaluation. Recently, it has articulated a clear understanding of the essential role of evaluation in government but has not advocated budget and staffing allocations to support it within the executive branch.

The Office of Management and Budget: A Continuing Search for Useful Information

Christopher G. Wye

The Office of Management and Budget (OMB) is the primary planning, policy-making, budget, and analytical support for the president as he manages the executive branch of government. OMB is staffed mainly by management and budget analysts who review and shape the government's program and budget to carry out the president's program in the most effective manner. OMB's view of the importance of evaluation—as reflected in its position toward the use of evaluation in department and agency management and budget preparation, its own use of evaluation work in the management of the executive branch and the preparation of the national budget, and its allocation of funding and staff for evaluation functions—is a powerful signal of the administration's view of the relative importance of evaluation in the overall management of the federal government.

Overview

Although OMB has responsibility for overall executive branch management and budget functions, its heaviest concentration of staff is on the budget side. The largest single concentration of staff—approximately 320 people, de-

---

The opinions expressed in this chapter are those of the author and do not necessarily represent or reflect the positions of the Department of Housing and Urban Development.

pending on how functions are classified—focuses predominantly on the budget. A smaller number, about 175, focus on things that might be classified as management-oriented. About 85 staff members serve in general administrative functions. In terms of influencing the budget, and of influencing management, to the considerable extent that it is driven by budgetary issues, the budget examiners wield the largest share of influence.

As a matter of internal organizational culture, the budget examiners see themselves as the "real OMB," and their work represents the irreducible center of the organization's activity. By law, the budget must be prepared every year and submitted to Congress. But while the budget examination function may wield the greatest influence within OMB, its ability to penetrate department and agency operations (in an evaluative or analytical sense) is limited. Primarily, this limitation is a result of a staffing imbalance: A handful of budget examiners must penetrate and decipher an agency budget assembled by hundreds of program specialists who have far greater expertise in its intricacies. The ability of budget examiners to assess a specific budget is largely limited to their own acquired expertise, the information in the budget proposal, on-the-shelf reports and studies, a limited number of requests for specific pieces of information, and whatever analysis can be done during the development of the budget document—a pressure-cooker-like process with a short fuse.

The 1980s

Throughout most of the 1980s, OMB showed very little interest in evaluation activity. A view emerged that evaluation is overly academic, expensive, unfocused, and largely irrelevant to practical management concerns; and that it is in fact part of the superstructure supporting entrenched, ineffective, inefficient, costly social programs. In 1983, OMB's director, David Stockman, effectively disenfranchised program evaluation in the federal government, gave a clear signal that evaluation was not wanted, and opened the door wide for departments and agencies to make budget and staffing cuts in the area of evaluation.

Stockman's signal was given by rescinding "Circular A-117: Management Improvement and the Use of Evaluation in the Executive Branch." The purpose of this circular was to "emphasize the importance of the role of evaluation in overall management improvement and the budget process." The circular established the policy, now revoked by the recision, that "all agencies of the Executive Branch of the Federal Government will assess the effectiveness of their programs and the efficiency with which they are conducted and seek improvement on a continuing basis so that Federal management will reflect the most progressive practices of both public and business management and result in improved service to the public."

"Circular A-117," while never receiving more than relatively weak support from either the executive or legislative branch of government, was a clear, strong articulation of the role of evaluation in federal management. In four pages of text, it clearly distinguished five types of evaluation activity (management improvement, management evaluation, program evaluation, performance measurement, and productivity assessment), required an annual report of management improvement and evaluation activities from each agency, and established for OMB a lead role in seeking ways to improve management through the use of evaluation. The withdrawal of the circular represented a clear withdrawal of OMB support for the evaluation function.

The withdrawal of this circular was not specifically aimed at evaluation. Rather, its intent was part of a broader campaign by OMB to reduce administrative burden on agencies. The evaluation circular was only one of several that were withdrawn simultaneously as a part of this broader initiative. However, it is a telling indication of the times that the withdrawal of support for evaluation was seen as a part of an initiative to reduce administrative burden—all the more so when it is recalled that one of the main functions of evaluation is to increase efficiency and effectiveness.

The withdrawal of support for program improvements that might be made through evaluation and analytical work was supplanted with a concern for management control. A government that was seen as out of control needed to be brought under control. The need for control was seen as so massive and immediate that the goal of improving performance was necessarily a secondary concern. Thus, throughout the 1980s, various initiatives sought to strengthen various aspects of control. The major management initiatives of the period reflected this concern: internal control; management control; fraud, waste, and mismanagement control; and fraud vulnerability assessment all sought to put boundaries on acceptable performance.

One of the outcomes of this view was that, consistently throughout the 1980s, staff and budget support declined for evaluation and other analytical functions aimed at improving performance, and simultaneously increased for control functions aimed at reinforcing legal, regulatory, and financial boundaries. Budget and staff for evaluation functions were reduced by 20 to 40 percent, and remaining evaluation activity was narrowed to administrative issues. Budgets and staff for inspectors general activity increased as agency-based inspectors general hired more auditors, accountants, and lawyers to root out fraud, waste, and mismanagement.

The Turn of the Decade

Beginning in the late 1980s, OMB began to show renewed interest in the role of evaluation in federal management. An effort was made to support the development and use of well-designed evaluation work in executive agencies and to look for information, analysis, and evaluation to inform the process of developing the budget.

As might have been expected, not much evaluation work was found, and what was found was of uneven quality. Whatever the reasons—the severe budget and staffing cuts of the 1980s, the tendency to focus more on internal administrative issues, and the academic emphasis of some evaluation activity—the lack of evaluation in general and the especially noteworthy lack of good examples of evaluation led OMB to believe that the evaluation capacity was so enervated as to require almost complete reconstitution. Lacking in-place working models of evaluation units and studies, a theoretical or conceptual framework for creating such units and studies de novo, and budget and staff resources to support their development, OMB attempted to piece together a practical strategy for supporting the use of program evaluation in the executive branch.

Soon after the 1988 election, informal feelers were sent out at the staff level within OMB to establish contact with evaluation practitioners within and close to the government, and to open a dialogue on what steps OMB should take to encourage the development of a competent evaluation capacity. Informal meetings with individuals and group discussions were held in a low-key atmosphere to solicit a wide range of views. As became apparent during this dialogue, OMB felt that there was little evaluation being done in the executive branch that could be endorsed as a model for the government as a whole, and that what was needed was an incremental approach of seeking out good evaluations and selectively calling for new evaluations in high-priority areas.

Within OMB, a number of steps were taken to support the use of evaluation. The budget analysis function began to build up its capacity to factor evaluation work into the budget review process. Agencies were encouraged to conduct evaluations and use them to support their budget submissions; and budget examiners were urged to request and use evaluations in their budget reviews. Some of the budget divisions revised their hiring practices to encourage the hiring of budget examiners with training in evaluation. Some encouraged examiners to actually carry out evaluations on their own in the "off (budget) season." In one division, a specific budget examiner was given the responsibility of coordinating evaluation work done by other budget examiners.

In 1990, OMB took its first step since 1972, when an existing unit focusing on evaluation was abolished, to reestablish a formal evaluation function within its own administrative structure. OMB created a new branch—the Evaluation, Planning, and Management by Objective (MBO) Branch—within the management side of the agency, with a staffing authorization of six people. The organization actually functions more like an internal management consulting operation, moving rapidly from one high-profile problem to another. Its focus is less on evaluation than on management improvement through the production of rapid analysis and recommendations on "hot issues."

This new emphasis on evaluation emerged in response to the rash of scandals associated with financial management that arose in the late 1980s, in part symbolized by the revelations of corruption at the Department of Housing and Urban Development. Based on the weaknesses exposed through the reporting requirements of the Federal Managers' Financial Integrity Act of 1982, OMB identified over one hundred high-risk areas susceptible to fraud, waste, and mismanagement. Basic responsibility for their correction rests with agency heads. But to address areas where the risk is exceptionally high, OMB has established "special weapons and tactics" (SWAT) teams to take immediate remedial action.

SWAT teams involve up to ten people, composed of staff from OMB and the agency concerned, and complete their work in two to three months. Review teams, a variant of the SWAT team approach, involve as many as ten to twenty people and take a longer period of time. The purpose of both groups is to tackle an immediate problem and put in place a remedial action plan. They reflect the administration's strategy of focusing on specific "fixes" for key problem areas. Since the inception of the SWAT and review team approach, the administration has initiated twenty joint agency-OMB reviews. In 1991, for example, a SWAT team sent into the Department of Education to look into $3.2 billion in student loan defaults led to a fourteen-point management improvement plan and new legislative proposals for making the program more efficient.

Despite its predominant focus on crisis management, the presence of the Evaluation, Planning, and MBO Branch gives the evaluation function a clear point of visibility, coordination, and leadership in the executive branch. Currently, developing congressional interest in the use of performance monitoring fits the overall OMB strategy of taking incremental, practical steps toward the reinstitution of program evaluation. Legislation is pending before Congress that supports the use of performance monitoring, especially the use of performance indicators. OMB favors the conceptual framework of this legislation but would prefer to see the results of planned demonstrations before the use of performance monitoring is required governmentwide. The branch has become a focal agent for tracking developments related to evaluation in government and represents the United States on the Public Management Panel of the Organization for Economic Cooperation and Development, which is just completing a major study of international experience with analytical techniques ranging from performance monitoring to program evaluation.

OMB's renewed interest in program evaluation has been formally expressed to the heads of executive departments and agencies in several ways. In 1989, a memo was issued to the executive branch asking for evaluation material that could be used in developing the budget. In 1990, a budget data request, a somewhat higher order of call in the OMB lexicon, was sent out, again asking for evaluation data for the next year's budget. And in 1991,

"Bulletin 91-13," an even higher order of call, was sent out, again requesting evaluation data for the budget process. "Bulletin 91-13" stands as the strongest countermeasure to the recision of "Circular A-117" in 1983, although a circular is still a higher order of directive than is a bulletin. The distinction between a circular and a bulletin is that the former is intended to establish a continuing direction, whereas a bulletin is intended to address an immediate issue.

Juxtaposed against "Circular A-117," "Bulletin 91-13" can only be seen as a beginning. Unlike the earlier circular, which emphasized the importance of evaluation in management and called on departments and agencies to use evaluation in a process of continuous management improvement, the new bulletin essentially asks for information on ongoing evaluations, planned evaluations that have not yet begun, and areas where evaluations are not yet planned but are needed. It does not so much support evaluation as it seeks information about work underway or about areas where additional work is needed.

This same cautious approach is evident in OMB's reaction to the proposed legislation calling for the use of performance monitoring throughout the government. Two bills introduced in 1991, S 20 and S 144D, require performance goals and standards to be established in all authorizing legislation, and OMB and agencies to develop performance indicators to monitor progress toward the goals. OMB's attitude toward these bills reflects a one-step-at-a-time, "let's see what works" approach. Instead of new legislation requiring governmentwide implementation of performance measures, OMB would prefer to see a sifting through of available experience to identify best practices, perhaps coupled with demonstrations of especially promising approaches.

OMB's implementation of the Chief Financial Officers Act of 1990 reflects the same concerns. In enacting the act, Congress created a deputy director for management in OMB to oversee the implementation of the statute. Subsequently, OMB has set up two offices under a new deputy director for management, the Office of Federal Financial Management with the predominant purpose of improving federal financial management, and the Office of General Management with the predominant purpose of improving management performance. OMB has specifically stipulated that the Office of General Management include in its responsibilities an evaluation function. Both purposes are to be achieved through performance reporting systems based on indicators of performance. Reflecting congressional intent, OMB's implementation of the statute has emphasized financial management. Its guidance to agencies emphasizes financial reporting, leaving performance reporting for a later stage of implementation when more is known about performance measurement systems.

In general, OMB has supported a range of activities that, while not specifically program evaluations, are nevertheless related to evaluation. The

1992 budget has the special section "Managing for Integrity and Efficiency," which includes such subtitles as "Improving Financial Management," "Improved Organizational Capacity," "Improved Information for Decision-making," and "Information Resources for Management." Taken together, these objectives recognize the importance of information for improved decision making and, ultimately, better program performance. They are constrained, however, by a continuing emphasis on information as a means for control rather than as a generator of improved performance. Embedded in the concept of performance improvement is the notion that the establishment of parameters of control is the beginning of better management, not the end.

Ultimately, maximum performance requires an analytical review and assessment of in-place program design, delivery, and impact for the purpose of increasing the effectiveness and efficiency of program operations. This review and assessment is the role performed by program evaluation. Mechanisms designed to establish management control provide clear boundaries for performance and improve performance only to the extent that they eliminate fraud, waste, and mismanagement. Functions that seek to evaluate program performance generate new ways of doing things at lower cost or with greater effectiveness. Under the assumption that programs are honestly and lawfully administered, program evaluation has the potential for generating additional cost savings or enhanced program impact, whereas control mechanisms add no net increment to the management equation.

OMB clearly understands the potential contribution that program evaluation can make to government operation. A specific section of the 1993 budget, titled "Improving Returns on Investment," is devoted almost exclusively to evaluation. This section is a clear, correct, detailed, and sophisticated definition of program evaluation and its utility. There is no fudging or dodging of definitional issues. There is a caution in the application of evaluation, but it is not unreasonable: "Evaluations of program results and performance should become an important (but not always prerequisite) factor in deciding program funding levels." No one would expect a deterministic approach to the use of evaluation in a system overlaid with a democratically elected political leadership.

OMB also recognizes the added importance of evaluation in a time of budget constraints. One could not hope for a stronger statement than the following (*Budget of the U.S. Government for Fiscal Year 1993,* 1992, p. 369): "Budget caps make it even more critical to plan for and conduct rigorous evaluations of programs, so that decisions to improve returns on investment can be more systematically based. The taxpayers deserve this much from their Government." The statement concludes with an even stronger call for the use of evaluation: "The Administration supports a systematic and sustained investment in more rigorous evaluation—as an aid to both the Executive Branch and the Congress in planning, monitoring, and assessing program results, and in determining future program needs. Evaluations include short-term and long-term efforts, comprehensive longitudinal outcome studies, and assessments of demonstrations or pilots" (1992, p. 369). OMB then lists nine priority evaluations to be conducted for the 1993 budget. The total funding of those evaluations for which cost estimates are available is $35 million.

As clarified in other chapters of this volume, the conclusion is inescapable that no matter how strongly OMB may support the use of evaluation in federal management or desire to use it in the development of the budget, the staff and budget resources—and, in some areas of the government, the capacity necessary to carry it out—are not there. Not in a decade has OMB articulated such a clear understanding of the discipline of program evaluation and of its potential for management improvement. And not in many decades has the need for evaluation been greater. As resources remain static or decline, more must be done with less. But not much can happen without direct budget support and agency capacity. All arguments about the need to move cautiously, to take practical, implementable steps notwithstanding, evaluation, like any other aspect of the federal management system, will respond to the incentives of the system itself; and when evaluation is given the same priority as other approaches to improving program operations, including a budget, a specific mission, and a mandate strong enough to empower it in the corridors of bureaucratic operations, it will provide a great return.

Reference

Budget of the United States Government for Fiscal Year 1993. Washington, D.C.: Government Printing Office, 1992.

CHRISTOPHER G. WYE is director of policy coordination in the Office of Community Planning and Development, U.S. Department of Housing and Urban Development. He is presently on an intergovernmental personnel assignment at the National Academy of Public Administration where he is staff director for a project on improving government performance through monitoring and program evaluation.

The Office of Personnel Management is responsible for overseeing the government's personnel management operations. Over the years it has searched for a workable balance between centralization and decentralization, oversight and encouragement, and subjective and objective approaches to management.

The Evolution of Federal Personnel Management Evaluation

Deborah Jordan

The Office of Personnel Management (OPM) under 5 U.S.C. 1104 has the responsibility to "establish and maintain an oversight program to ensure that activities under any authority" delegated to OPM or to agency heads from OPM "are in accordance with the merit system principles and standards established" by OPM. The means by which OPM, and previously the Civil Service Commission (CSC), has accomplished this mandate has evolved over the years. Since the establishment of CSC's Inspection Division over forty-five years ago, there has been a struggle to balance the responsibilities of the evaluation program: to oversee agency compliance with law, rules, and regulations; to provide personnel management information to management and agencies to assist with decision making; and to improve the state of personnel management in agencies. This balance has often shifted, emphasizing one responsibility over the other. However, all continue to be overseen by the OPM evaluation program.

Evaluation: The Early Years

The evaluation function of CSC, called "inspections," had its inception during World War II. Before that time, personnel management was centralized at CSC. But with the dramatic growth in the size of the government during World War II, CSC was forced to decentralize its operations and delegate personnel management authority to agencies.

The opinions expressed in this chapter are those of the author and do not necessarily represent or reflect the positions of the Office of Personnel Management.

This delegation of authority created the need to review, or "inspect," agency compliance. In 1945, Executive Order 9830 made personnel management the primary responsibility of department and agency heads and required an "adequate system of inspections" to ensure compliance. These inspections were the responsibility of the Inspection Division, later termed the Bureau of Inspections.

Over the years, the inspections function has been redefined to coincide with changing needs and priorities. But, in general, it has moved along a series of continua from compliance to assistance, from personnel administration to organizational performance, from installation-specific to departmentwide assessments, from unstandardized to standardized approaches, from inspection only to inspection and audit reviews, and from less to more sophisticated analytical approaches. As the central agency in a decentralized system, OPM's essential task has been to strike a balance between oversight and assistance.

During the mid-1970s, a study was conducted within CSC to examine the governmentwide personnel management evaluation program. It is noteworthy that comments received from both evaluators and agency personnelists revealed a significant disparity of views on the goals and purposes of the evaluation program. Some commented that the program was exclusively for ensuring agencies' compliance with regulations. Others saw the evaluation program's role as that of "selling" current CSC programs. The conclusion was that most views recognized multiple objectives: enforcement of compliance, joint efforts to bring about individual program improvements, and information gathering and sharing. The multiple objectives reflected the spirit of the original charter of the inspections program.

These multiple objectives remain a central part of the evaluation program, although the balance often shifts direction depending on a variety of variables, some within OPM's control and others not. Even with the changes in the evaluation program in the 1950s (programmatic versus individual action reviews) and in the 1960s (total personnel management versus personnel administration), agencies still perceive the evaluation program as primarily compliance-oriented. Beyond legal compliance, agencies express confusion about the standards applied by CSC in reviewing the components of personnel management. Agencies view CSC's role as advisory, except for compliance and enforcement authority. This points to the fact that agency management has the responsibility to improve personnel management, separate from CSC's evaluation program.

Civil Service Reform Act of 1978

Jimmy Carter's campaign for the presidency included a major policy agenda of "cleaning up the mess in Washington." The personnel management system was viewed as overly complex, cumbersome, excessively bureaucratic, and largely ineffective (Merit Systems Protection Board, 1989). As president, Carter appointed civil service commissioners whose primary objective was the decentralization of personnel management authorities to line managers, who actually perform the work of the federal government.

The Civil Service Reform Act of 1978 (CSRA, P.L. 95-454) became law on October 13, 1978. The purpose of the law was simply stated: "to provide the people of the United States with a competent, honest, and productive Federal work force reflective of the Nation's diversity, and to improve the quality of public service." It was the first major reform of the federal civil service in nearly one hundred years.

Two reorganization plans followed the CSRA. One plan abolished CSC and divided its principal functions between the Office of Personnel Management (OPM) and the Merit Systems Protection Board. The Federal Labor Relations Authority (FLRA) was also established, replacing the Federal Labor Relations Council. OPM would assume the leadership role in public personnel management policy; MSPB and its independent Office of Special Counsel would resolve employee appeals, safeguard the merit system, and protect whistleblowers; and FLRA would deal with labor-management issues. The other plan assigned the Equal Employment Opportunity Commission leadership responsibility in the federal government for matters pertaining to equal employment opportunities.

The CSRA brought many new initiatives that OPM was assigned to implement. These initiatives covered the spectrum of personnel management issues: delegation of personnel management authorities, creation of the Senior Executive Service, performance appraisal and merit pay, personnel research and demonstration projects, executive management and development, labor-management relations, establishment of the Intergovernmental Personnel Program, productivity improvement, and many others.

The reform came with a strategy for a five-year evaluation of implementation efforts. The evaluation plan essentially had three components: (1) Program plans for evaluating specific reform initiatives—for example, the Senior Executive Service, merit pay, and the new performance appraisal system—included the use of case studies, special studies, and management information generated by OPM program offices. (2) Organizational assessment studies, conducted by university-based teams under contract with OPM, were to be done on the implementation efforts and the effects of select initiatives at about a dozen sites over a five-year span. (3) A Federal Employee Attitude Survey was designed to obtain federal employees' perceptions about the reforms and their effects (General Accounting Office, 1981).

Practically every major program group at OPM worked on the CSRA evaluation. The evaluation program office, now called the Office of Agency Compliance and Evaluation (ACE), was no exception. For the first few years following CSRA implementation, traditional evaluations of agencies' personnel programs and regulatory compliance were also supplemented with efforts to monitor and assist in agency implementation of reform initiatives. During the late 1970s, the Agency Relations unit was created to work closely with federal departments and agencies to identify and solve particular personnel problems. Agency Relations officers worked as personnel consultants and provided significant information about the implementation efforts from the agency perspective. The other result of this new unit was conflict with ACE.

The late 1970s were difficult years for ACE. Much of its technical assistance role, in full operation before the CSRA, was diminished because of the required compliance reviews and the case studies done to monitor CSRA implementation. The Agency Relations unit essentially took over that role, and the conflict of function already existing between the Agency Relations unit and ACE was amplified—policeman versus advocate.

The Devine Years

With the new Reagan administration came interesting changes to OPM's evaluation program. The downsizing that was occurring in OPM after the CSRA was further compounded by a personnel reduction in early 1982. The ACE evaluation resources went from a high of 237.5 full-time equivalents (FTEs) in fiscal year 1980 to a low of 121 FTEs in fiscal year 1986. The current program has resources of 133 FTEs nationwide and is holding steady. Other changes occurred when the OPM director, Donald J. Devine, decided to restructure the evaluation program.

Devine saw a program that was still based at the installation level. These findings could not be addressed to even the agencywide level, much less be indicative of governmentwide trends. The current program did not attempt to generate information about personnel management in any systematic way. The director did not see the utility of the current program for providing information that would help mold OPM policy on personnel issues—what he perceived to be the true function of OPM. What resulted from his vision was a statistically based evaluation program was limited on-site work.

In 1984, OPM initiated a statistically oriented approach for identifying agency and governmentwide concerns in need of top agency and OPM management attention. The emphasis was on identifying systemic federal personnel problems, along with ensuring regulatory compliance. The new methodology called for the compilation of installation data from the Central Personnel Data File on position management, position classification, staffing, performance management, and personnel administration practices. ACE evaluators would conduct short one- to two-day reviews at every installation with at least fifty employees. This original plan would have encompassed over four thousand installations. In fiscal year 1986, OPM modified the site definition to include only installations with one hundred or more employees. This decrease in installation assessment visits (IAVs) was the result of reductions in evaluation staff and money. The coverage was very intense—the five-year period involved approximately thirty-five hundred IAVs covering nearly 90 percent of the total federal work force. Other components of the revised approach included generation of a personnel management indicators report and a series of issue analyses.

The indicators report remains one of the principal mechanisms that OPM uses to evaluate agencies on their overall personnel management performance. It is prepared for each of the twenty-two largest agencies, which encompass over 90 percent of the federal population, and includes statistical indicators covering position classification and management, staffing, and performance management. Specific indicators include employee turnover, standard average grade, and minority representation. OPM now has seven years of longitudinal data on the twenty-two agencies. These data allow significant analyses of trends in the major indicators. At the time of the project's inception, it was considered a means of seeing "big picture" personnel management concerns, and a means of showing agencies how their personnel programs compare, in a statistically valid way, with the rest of the federal government.

During the five-year evaluation period, OPM intended to do twenty issue analyses, four each year. Each analysis was designed to be a comprehensive study of a governmentwide personnel management issue and would include visits to about one hundred agency installations. According to the plan, at the end of the five years the OPM director would have a clear picture of federal personnel management. The first year, four analyses were completed: Governmentwide Management of Position Classification and Position Management Programs; Personnel Administration Efficiency, Costs, and Services; Effectiveness of the Government's Appointing System; and Effectiveness of the Performance Appraisal System for Non–Merit Pay Employees. No other issue analyses were conducted past the first year. Other reviews included ACE participation in agency-led reviews, which are conducted by the agency with participation by OPM evaluators. Also, targeted installation reviews were done at the discretion of the OPM regional directors at installations within their regions that had significant personnel management problems. Both of these types of reviews continue to be part of the evaluation program.

During the five-year evaluation cycle, there was a new director of OPM. Constance Horner did not change much about the evaluation program and came to realize that it could be useful to OPM by providing information to the OPM program offices for policy formulation. However, outside forces, namely Congress, the General Accounting Office, and the Merit Systems Protection Board were critical of OPM's program because of the concern that the evaluation function was not meeting its primary obligation (under 5

U.S.C. 1104) of ensuring agency compliance with law, rules, and regulations. There was a need for a new program—beyond the statistically based IAVs—to try to achieve greater balance among the evaluation function's three roles: helper, police, and informer.

Fiscal Year 1989 and Beyond

The new program was founded on the idea that OPM should target its evaluation strategy at the three levels involved in federal personnel management: individual installations, agencies, and the federal government as a whole. Prior to the CSRA, the installation level was the evaluation program's primary focus. After the CSRA, the balance shifted to trying to address governmentwide concerns. Additionally, the evaluation function emerged from the post-CSRA period with evaluators who were computer literate and versed in statistical methodology. The earlier shift to data analysis was continued in the new program and has since been institutionalized.

This time, ACE structured the five-year evaluation cycle, targeting on-site work at installations with five hundred or more employees. Installations with less than five hundred are also reviewed using an off-site, statistically based methodology. The major components of the program address the three levels of personnel management: governmentwide reviews (GWRs), which address personnel management issues from a nationwide perspective; agency-specific reviews, which address personnel management concerns at the agency level; and targeted installation reviews, which review specified problems at an individual installation.

The first issues covered under the GWR process included typical personnel management issues such as the impact of increased delegations of authority, recruitment and retention of clerical employees, and performance management. Additionally, OPM's director was interested in gathering information on workplace issues such as employees assistance programs, agency AIDS programs, dependent care and employee health and fitness programs. In keeping with our legal responsibility, ACE also reviewed agency compliance with regulations and OPM requirements on a variety of personnel authorities. ACE visited about 180 installations nationwide during the first year of the program. Each review included specific feedback to the head of each installation. The information was then compiled by each region and ultimately summarized into eight reports reflecting the governmentwide findings.

In years since the fiscal year 1989 program, the GWRs have focused on different personnel issues. After the first year, ACE solicited input from agencies and program offices about which personnel management issues they wanted to see reviewed. Many suggestions came in, though ultimately it was OPM management's decision. Fiscal year 1990 included timely issues: recruitment and retention, training and development, incentive awards, special emphasis programs such as the Federal Equal Opportunity Recruitment Program, as well as delegations of personnel management authority. Additionally, the evaluation program has continued to make regulatory compliance part of its evaluation program. Fiscal year 1991 looked at staffing timeliness of personnel action and issues related to implementation of the Federal Employee Pay Comparability Act of 1990 (FEPCA).

One of the most significant improvements in the evaluation program has been the development of the agency analyst network. Started in 1986, the agency analyst network has improved under the new program. All evaluators (now called agency analysts), both in headquarters and in OPM's five regions, have specific agency assignments. Agency analysts identify, analyze, and seek to resolve problems and other issues specific to their departments and agencies. Their work involves direct interaction with agency staff to seek resolution of personnel management problems, to explore ways of otherwise enhancing the agency's personnel program effectiveness, and to share general information. Within OPM, the network facilitates coordinated gathering and reporting of information, including emerging concerns within agencies about personnel management policy as well as exemplary practices for export to other agencies. Essentially, the agency analyst concept combines the functions of the former role of agency officers with the evaluator role.

Another aspect of the evaluation program, which is encouraged by the agency analyst network, is the agency-specific review. These reviews are addressed to the particular personnel management concerns of a specific agency. Recent reviews have included *Recruitment and Workforce Development at the Department of Energy, National Park Service: Use of Seasonal and Temporary Employees,* and *Internal Revenue Service: The Agency's Efforts to Recruit, Develop, and Maintain a Quality Work Force.* These tailored reviews either address an issue that OPM sees within an agency (for example, the National Park Service's use of temporaries) or offer assistance at an agency's request.

The resources required to fulfill the GWR agenda at each installation visited (eight agendas in fiscal year 1989 and seven in fiscal year 1990) generally precluded significant expansion of these reviews to cover other installation-specific issues in need of attention. The GWR agendas were also tied to the schedule, beginning at the same time each year and concluding in time for the findings to be provided to ACE by the end of the fiscal year. This scheduling was creating problems; specifically, the time available for on-site work was short, resulting in compressed scheduling of the reviews and less opportunity to arrange cooperative reviews with agency-internal personnel management evaluation staff. Also, ACE was forced to analyze and report GWR findings while finalizing guidance and agendas for the upcoming year, which was impeding both processes. ACE management decided to alter elements of the program to address these concerns.

Fiscal year 1992 brought a restructured evaluation program. Already in fiscal year 1991, ACE provided assistance for several OPM policy initiatives by gathering information for use in assessing agency implementation of the new FEPCA authorities. Additional policy assistance is now occurring in fiscal year 1992 through continued monitoring of FEPCA authorities and, for the first several months of the year, review of work and family life programs. There is the possibility of a major new agenda of performance management. This "rolling agenda" concept has been introduced, which essentially frees fiscal year constraints for the planning and conduct of reviews. Agendas will be added to the on-site reviews throughout the year (the potential performance management review), and on-site information will be gathered until a sufficient number of installation evaluations have been conducted to develop governmentwide findings.

Additionally, the review agendas have been left open ended to allow individual agency analysts the opportunity to tailor the review to the installation. These "enhanced reviews" will achieve two purposes: ACE will continue to gather governmentwide information for OPM policymakers through specified agendas, and individual installations will receive better personnel management coverage as the evaluator designs specific agendas for use at that particular installation.

Another important development of the past several years has been the increasing role of technical assistance in the evaluation program. Fostered by the agency analyst network, agencies are now viewing ACE as a source of assistance with personnel management concerns. These requests come from all sources. In her round of visits at the beginning of her term, Director Constance Newman offered OPM's assistance. Secretary of Energy James D. Watkins took her up on the offer, and ACE, in conjunction with OPM executive training and recruitment program offices, conducted a comprehensive study of Energy's recruitment, training, and succession planning programs. A request from management at the Peace Corps brought ACE in for a personnel management review and resulted in a senior manager going on detail for six months to assist with implementation of the recommended changes in the personnel program. Other assistance has included guidance to agency operating personnel offices for improving systems and Intergovernmental Personnel Act assignments for project-oriented work on a variety of personnel management issues.

Additionally, ACE has developed internal sources for technical assistance. OPM releases the *Digest of Exemplary Personnel Practices,* which essentially summarizes a number of innovative personnel practices that agencies have developed and ACE has identified during its installation visits as particularly noteworthy and potentially useful to other installations. Agencies that are highlighted agree to provide information to interested installations. Also, ACE has established a clearinghouse of information on personnel management evaluation for agencies to use in improving their internal programs.

Conclusion

A wise man once said, "You've got to see where you've been, to know where you're going." This adage holds true for the evaluation function at OPM as well. Historically, the Civil Service Commission and OPM have been bound by 5 U.S.C. 1104, which established responsibility for oversight of personnel management. That oversight function has been translated into three program objectives: assisting agencies in improving their personnel programs; ensuring that agency personnel programs operate within law, regulation, and OPM guidance; and providing significant findings on agency personnel programs and trends to the director and other OPM program offices for their use in setting policy.

There has been a shifting balance among these three objectives. The balance has been, and always will be, affected by OPM management, agencies, and political concerns. The evaluation program has shifted emphases many times over the years. However, the current program shows the greatest potential yet. The agency analyst network, combined with the yearly evaluation program, is as close to a perfect balance of these program objectives as has ever been achieved.

References

General Accounting Office. "Obstacles Hamper the Office of Personnel Management's Evaluation of the Implementation of the 1978 Civil Service Reform Act." Letter to Donald J. Devine, Director, U.S. Office of Personnel Management, Sept. 14, 1981.

Merit Systems Protection Board. *Federal Personnel Management Since Civil Service Reform.* Washington, D.C.: Government Printing Office, 1989.

DEBORAH JORDAN is senior agency analyst in the Office of Agency Compliance and Evaluation, U.S. Office of Personnel Management.

Over time, the General Services Administration evaluation functions have been decentralized throughout the management structure and have become more sharply focused on management issues, partly in response to cuts in budget and personnel.

Evaluation in the General Services Administration: Adapting for Greater Efficiency and Utility

Caleb Kriesberg

As the federal government's primary manager of government property, the General Services Administration (GSA) is constantly concerned with the cost and quality of services rendered to the government.

Organization and Structure of Evaluation

The GSA is one of the federal government's main business managers. It is organized into four services: Federal Supply, Federal Property Resources, Public Buildings, and Information Resources Management. Evaluation in the broadest sense is practiced by the managers in the services whenever they judge the suitability of a contract, the adequacy of a building, or the quality of equipment. But evaluation as program or mission assessment is centered in three of the agency's offices outside the services: Office of the Inspector General, Office of Administration, and Office of the Chief Financial Officer.

The agency's inspector general, like all inspectors general, is a member of the President's Council on Integrity and Efficiency. The Office of the Inspector General manages the agency's internal audit function and conducts both external and internal evaluation. There are regional inspectors general for auditing and for investigations located at each of GSA's regional headquarters. The Office of Administration includes the largest number and greatest diversity of evaluation functions in GSA. The office is the GSA's liaison for General Accounting Office (GAO) audits and is an important reviewer of inspector general audits. It includes, in part, the Office of Management Controls and Evaluation, the Personnel Office, and the Office of Quality Management and Training. The Office of the Chief Financial Officer functions to ensure that proper financial controls are in place to achieve compliance with the congressionally mandated Chief Financial Officers Act of 1991. This act requires that financial monitoring and reporting systems be established and that regular reports be prepared to track agency handling of financial accounts.

Other areas of the agency also relate to or employ the evaluation function. The Office of Policy Analysis, at the direction of GSA's administrator, is not involved directly with program evaluation but deals with policy analysis and assessment, and with management reform and planning for the agency as a whole that reflect the result of the agency's evaluations. It also deals with policy issues at the agency level and among the agency, other agencies, and the executive branch in general. The Office of Ethics and Civil Rights can advise managers on ethics as it pertains to evaluation and the issues of fraud and abuse.

Evolution of Evaluation in the GSA: 1980–1991

In the 1980s, due in part to the Reagan administration's interest in reducing the size of the federal government and to the federal government's attempt to reduce the federal deficit, the size and budget of GSA became smaller. From 1982 to 1991, the agency went from about thirty thousand to about twenty thousand employees. The GSA moved many of its evaluation functions through different offices and titles, in part in response to reduction in resources but also in response to changing views of evaluation and changing needs and interests of new managers. For example, in the 1980s, changes in the leadership of the agency immediately led to the replacement of one evaluation office with another. Much of this change is summarized in Table 11.1.

During the past decade, the agency added the Office of the Chief Financial Officer and the Office of Administration. It also established, and abolished, the Office of Oversight, the Office of Policy and Management Systems, and the Office of Management Services, all of which had evaluation functions (see Table 11.1). Over time, the main seat of the evaluation function came to be not an office by itself but rather a part of the Office of Administration: the Office of Management Controls and Evaluation.

Facets of Evaluation in the GSA

To many people in GSA, the main purpose of evaluation has changed from regulatory monitoring and enforcement to assistance, but the oversight function remains rigorous and widely practiced through the agency. Follow-

Table 11.1. Evolution of Evaluation in the GSA, 1974–1991

Year	*Events*
1974	Civil Service Commission (now Office of Personnel Management) directs agencies to evaluate their personnel
1975	GSA Office of Personnel establishes branch of full-time personnel evaluators (this branch is later disbanded)
1976	GSA establishes Office of Policy, Planning, and Evaluation
1978	Congress establishes Office of Inspector General
	GSA establishes Offices of Inspector General
1979	GSA abolishes Office of Policy, Planning, and Evaluation
1981	GSA establishes Office of Administration
	GSA establishes Office of Policy and Management Systems
	GSA establishes Office of Oversight (for evaluation)
1982	OMB passes Federal Managers' Financial Integrity Act
1983	GSA transfers Office of Oversight to Office of Policy and Management Systems (gives that office evaluation function)
	Federal government in process of broad personnel and budget cuts
1985	GSA abolishes Office of Policy and Management Systems (and with it the Office of Oversight)
	GSA establishes Office of Audit Resolution and Internal Controls (for evaluation) in Office of Administration
1986	GSA establishes Office of Management Services in Office of Administration
	GSA abolishes Office of Audit Resolution and Internal Controls and transfers its functions to Office of Management Services
1990	Congress passes Chief Financial Officers Act
	GSA abolishes Office of Management Services
	GSA establishes Office of Management Controls and Evaluation (for evaluation) in Office of Administration
	Federal government directs agencies to have Total Quality Management training
	GSA establishes Office of Quality Management Training in Office of Administration
	GSA establishes Management Control and Oversight Council (a committee to provide leadership and oversight on GSA evaluation)
1991	GSA establishes Office of the Chief Financial Officer

ing repeated reductions in resources, evaluation is now carried out mainly by individual programs, with program managers themselves deciding on and sometimes actually carrying out their own evaluations; and there is a general satisfaction with this approach. However, broader-scale evaluation is carried out in response to congressional statutory requirements. The range is from small-scale, episodic, specific studies conducted by program managers to large-scale, statutorily required, annual reports to Congress.

In the remainder of this chapter, I describe three congressionally mandated evaluation functions and one form of internally generated evaluation, customer feedback. I then describe GSA evaluation as it has developed in four units of the agency. Finally, I briefly consider trends in evaluation in GSA.

Kinds of Evaluation

In GSA, evaluation activity is generated in connection with the following kinds of functions: inspector general reviews, the Federal Managers' Financial Integrity Act, "Circular A-123" on review of internal control, "Circular A-127" on review of financial management systems, Total Quality Management, and customer feedback evaluation.

Inspector General Reviews. The GSA Office of Inspector General, established by public law in 1978, serves to combat potential fraud, corruption, and mismanagement. The Office of Audits in the Office of Inspector General prepares annual audit plans. Each year, the inspector general asks GSA commissioners to offer suggestions—candidate topics or programs—for the audit plan. The inspector general considers these suggestions together with those generated by his or her own staff and prepares a final audit plan. There are two types of inspector general audits at GSA: management or program audits, which are often called *internal audits;* and contract audits, which are often called *external audits.* External audits ask whether GSA is getting the best possible deals from vendors.

Federal Managers' Financial Integrity Act (FMFIA). The FMFIA, mandated by the Office of Management and Budget (OMB) in 1982, requires an agency to send an annual statement to Congress and the president. Basically, the statement must report on the problems facing the agency and what it is doing to correct them. OMB and GAO also see the statement.

This statement by an agency is required by OMB "Circular A-123: Review of Internal Control Systems," which includes an annual assurance statement process and a management control improvement program, the latter for detailed review. These items include vulnerability assessments and the search for material control weaknesses, serious flaws that program managers would want to find and report. Through them, program managers evaluate the potential weaknesses of their own program components. For example, in the Federal Supply Service of GSA, there is a personal property sales component, a utilization/donation component, and an excess property component. The last involves the way that the service manages donations of excess property to states and eligible donees.

Another OMB directive, "Circular A-127," requires a review of financial management systems and is a form of internal control review or evaluation that is financially oriented. It might be the basis for a review of the automatic data-processing system as it bears on financial matters. Data and information systems, as they relate to financial tracking and reporting, have been the target of several GAO audits of agency operations.

Total Quality Management. In 1990, the federal government encouraged all agencies to adopt Total Quality Management (TQM), a philosophy for enhancing quality, timeliness, and customer satisfaction. GSA responded by creating the Office of Quality Management and Training within the Office of Administration. This office promotes program leadership and training. In addition, every GSA service has at least one lead person overseeing TQM activities. This philosophy relates to evaluation because it involves judging how managers can perform their missions better, improve their processes, and better serve their clients, internally and externally.

Customer Feedback Evaluation. Customer feedback evaluation, or customer satisfaction assessment, is not required by either legislative statute or executive branch directive. It is something that goes on in different forms in each of the services, and in other areas of the agency, as a way that units determine how well they are accomplishing their respective service goals. For the Personnel Office, the customers are GSA's own employees. The office sends out questionnaires or surveys to learn about the timeliness of its hiring for different offices in the agency, and its performance in other aspects of its mission. For the services, the customers are individuals, agencies, and organizations in federal government service throughout the country.

The Federal Supply Service, for example, employs surveys, quality hotlines, user panels, computerized interagency communication (Multi-Use File for Interagency News), and visits from customer service directors to gauge the interests, preferences, and satisfaction of customers. The problem is challenging because GSA customers are so diverse. Who is the customer? Who uses the services? A fire ranger on a mountain in Montana or a whole naval shipyard may order supplies. Who is eventually using them? GSA is continually looking for better methods to conduct surveys to determine customer satisfaction for its services.

Examples of GSA Units Doing Evaluation

The types of evaluation being done by GSA units is illustrated by the work of the Office of the Inspector General, the Office of Management Controls and Evaluation, the Personnel Office, and the Management Control Oversight Council.

Office of Inspector General. Since its founding the GSA Office of Inspector General has gone through several changes, some due to budget and personnel cuts. There was a reduction in employees from 580 to 330 from 1982 to 1985, and Congress required an 8 percent across-the-board budget cut that affected the office. During this time, an acting inspector general was in place, and new agency managers were not familiar with the office's functions. The office responded to cuts in staffing and funding by emphasizing contract audits (audits of external contracts) as opposed to program audits (audits of internal programs). At that time, the ratio of contract audits to program audits was about 60 percent to 40 percent. Later, with the appointment of a permanent inspector general and restored funding and staffing levels, the ratio of contract to program audits stabilized at 50 percent each. In order to more sharply focus internal evaluation within the Office of the Inspector General, the office's internal evaluation function was made a part of the inspector general's immediate staff.

Office of Management Controls and Evaluation. The Office of Management Controls and Evaluation, in the Office of Administration, is the major administrative control function outside the Office of the Inspector General. It functions as the department's liaison to GAO. In this capacity, it coordinates GSA input to and comments on evaluations and studies of the agency by GAO. It also manages GSA compliance with FMFIA "Circular A-123." And it is a major partner with the inspector general in following up with program managers to correct problems identified in inspector general audits and reports. These functions were transferred to the Office of Administration after the evaluation function was abolished within GSA as a free-standing operation.

Personnel Office. The Personnel Office, also within the Office of Administration, must evaluate its personnel programs in compliance with the *Federal Personnel Manual* produced by the Office of Personnel Management. The Personnel Office checks, for example, to see if promotions are done appropriately, if positions are classified accurately, and if position descriptions are current. Before the 1980s, these reviews were frequently performed on-site. More recently, there have been fewer resources for on-site reviews by personnel specialists in the different regions. An automated personnel system has given the Personnel Office much valuable information; its statistics give valuable clues about what is happening in personnel procedures. Personnel sends out questionnaires, surveys, and emphasizes self-evaluation at the program level. The office has also found it valuable to focus priorities on a few programs, which are examined in depth rather than in terms of broad coverage.

Management Control Oversight Council. The GSA Management Control Oversight Council was established in 1990 to allow senior managers in GSA to provide leadership and policy oversight regarding the implementation of the FMFIA and OMB "Circular A-123." It reviews the agency's own annual management control plan, in which offices and regions prepare evaluations for GSA. The council consists of the deputy administrator, the associate administrator for administration, the associate administrator for acquisition policy, and the chief financial officer, with the inspector general as ex-officio adviser and the director of the Office of Management Controls and Evaluation as support staff. The council helps coordinate GSA's diverse activities in evaluation.

Trends in Evaluation in GSA

There have been a variety of trends in evaluation at GSA over the past decade. Partly in response to budget and personnel cuts, GSA evaluators have been learning new strategies. Surveys and questionnaires have become increasingly important, as have computerized data and statistics. Self-evaluation at the program level has become more emphasized, as there are fewer personnel available to go to different regions or offices. At the same time, with fewer personnel, offices have been abolished or consolidated, the evaluation function has been focused in fewer locations organizationally, reviews by offices dealing with evaluation have been focused on particular programs, and an effort has been made to coordinate the diverse evaluation activities. GSA has thus far been able to avoid duplication by having reviews for one federal requirement also serve for another and by encouraging coordination and sharing of information among the different evaluation activities.

Caleb Kriesberg is an instructor at the Comprehensive Instructional Center, University of the District of Columbia, Washington, D.C.

Evaluation specialists and auditors are working side by side to improve program performance. Auditors concentrate on comparing a condition against a criterion; evaluators concentrate on what has occurred, estimating what would have occurred without the program and comparing the two situations to determine program effects.

Expanding Evaluation Capabilities in the General Accounting Office

Eleanor Chelimsky

Social scientists and auditors are working together to strengthen program evaluation capabilities at the General Accounting Office (GAO). For some time now, we at GAO have been expanding our ability to do program evaluation. By program evaluation, I mean the use of systematic research methods to assess policy or program design, implementation, and effectiveness. We began building this capability informally throughout the 1970s in our Program Analysis Division and then took the formal step, in 1980, of creating the Institute for Program Evaluation. In 1983, this unit became GAO's Program Evaluation and Methodology Division (PEMD).

Types of Evaluation

The chief purpose of PEMD is to help us address the kinds of complex and technically demanding problems that congressional committees are increasingly asking us to resolve. Since the questions involved concern nearly every aspect of the policy or program process, from formulation through execution to assessment, we had to develop an evaluation capacity in all these areas. Three kinds of evaluations were required of us: (1) assessing a policy or program still in the design phase (for example, informing Congress on

---

The opinions expressed in this chapter are those of the author and do not necessarily represent or reflect the positions of the General Accounting Office. This chapter is reprinted, with permission, with minor revisions from the *GAO Journal*, Winter/Spring 1990, pp. 43-52.

whether enough evidence was available to support a particular policy on AIDS or a program for homeless people); (2) measuring program or policy implementation (for example, identifying the quality of medical care given Medicaid patients or the initial results of efforts by states to establish enterprise zones); and (3) establishing the actual effects achieved by a policy or program (for example, determining the impact of "back-to-basics" educational reforms on student performance or the effects of sewage treatment plants on level of water pollution). Further, because of GAO's role as "the evaluators' evaluator," we had a fourth task: critiquing the soundness of the evidence reported to Congress by others on program or policy design, implementation, and effectiveness.

Demonstrating Methodological Capabilities

Evaluation typically examines the world through a rearview mirror. It asks such questions as the following: What happened as a result of implementing this new policy? Did it make a difference? If so, can it be measured? Would we have seen the same effect if the policy had never been put in place? Since, by and large, evaluation methods have been developed in this retrospective mode, approaches have long existed that allow an evaluation to assess a policy or program that has been on going for some time. So, in 1980, we could feel relatively confident about evaluation's ability to assess program policy implementation and effectiveness. It was uncommon in 1980, however, to encounter an evaluation that looked forward, that asked prospective questions such as the following: What effects, if any, can we expect in the future from implementing this proposed program? Does its design make sense? Is it powerful enough to bring about the effects that people say it will have? Does the problem addressed by the program warrant the expenditure requested?

Looking into the Future

To deal with prospective questions, we developed an approach that we call the *prospective evaluation synthesis*. We tried this approach for the first time in 1985 to evaluate program designs proposed by two bills introduced in Congress that year, both of which addressed the problem of teenage pregnancy. Since then, we have used the method several times and are continuing to vary or expand it as we apply it to different topic areas. We have also employed forecasting and other methods of projection to estimate the future effects of programs or policies.

Congressional staff have most frequently asked us for evaluations of program or policy effectiveness. This was predictable; it is the area in which evaluation first established its reputation, and requests for this type of evaluation have come in since we formally established our evaluation capacity in 1980. On the other hand, requests for evaluations of program or policy design have been more common in recent years, largely because it is only since 1985 that we felt prepared to deal with prospective issues.

Central Trend

Based on congressional interest, this type of forward-looking work seems likely to increase over the next few years. There are several reasons. First, prospective studies allow evaluation to make a policy contribution embodying the best available information, at a point in the program process when agendas are not set, bureaucracies are not yet in place, and rational discussion is still likely to be acceptable. This situation contrasts with evaluations of effectiveness, for example, which come after the fact and tend to elicit, first, apprehension and, later, outraged cries from those whose careers may be affected by the negative findings. This is not to argue, of course, that effectiveness evaluations should be avoided; merely that they present bigger "people" obstacles than do prospective studies. Second, program advocates in Congress and in the executive branch can obtain expert design assistance for their new proposals at a time when they may want to convince other policymakers of their program's likely success. Finally, the evaluation of program design performs a service either when it strengthens programs that are not optimally structured or when it validates the basic soundness of what is to be undertaken.

Methodological Critiques

Methodological critiques have been much requested by Congress, second only to effectiveness evaluations. PEMD has used methodological criteria in several different ways: to develop a framework for assessing threats to validity, to examine the relationships between particular study aspects (for example, sample size or data analysis) and conclusions drawn by the study reviewed, and to reanalyze data and conduct case studies to determine the methodological quality of evaluation conclusions. When an individual topic area is so complex that the application of methodological criteria requires special substantive knowledge, we ask expert panels to help bring substantive and methodological criteria together.

Working for the Legislative Branch

In adapting executive branch evaluation practices for congressional users, we found that we did indeed need to change our procedures. Timeliness with regard to legislative milestones turned out to be a critically important consideration dictated by the way in which the Congress works. Coming in with a report when the debate is over and the vote has been tallied is not just a problem, it can be a kind of obliteration—the equivalent of not having done a study at all. Yet, some evaluation methods, for example, a comparative design with original data collection, take a long time, often between two and three years. As a result, we developed or adapted methods to produce answers to legislative questions more quickly while maintaining acceptable quality levels. Our general procedures for working with Congress also evolved. Three features now take into account the special problem of legislative time constraints.

First, we do not begin a study until we have reached a precise understanding with the congressional sponsor of the information need that the study must address. (This need is not always obvious or straightforward.) Second, we communicate often with the sponsor to ensure that he or she knows how the work is progressing, what the products will be, when it will arrive, and how the legislative questions will be answered. Finally, we look for new ways to answer legislative questions only if time constraints preclude the use of more traditional methods.

Three Fast-Track Approaches

For situations in which time is short, we have developed three fast-track approaches.

Evaluation Synthesis. We began developing this method in 1980 to respond to legislative sponsors who need effectiveness studies under time frames that are too brief for us to collect original data. The method is used only when a sponsor is willing to accept an analysis of existing studies as a substitute for new research. The evaluation synthesis determines what is known in the topic area, assesses the strength and weaknesses of the various studies that constitute its data base, and identifies any gaps in the needed information. Six to nine months are usually required for this type of study, as opposed to the two to three years needed for an effectiveness evaluation. The twenty-six congressionally requested syntheses completed to date by PEMD are a reflection of our sponsors' regard for their usefulness.

Use of Extant Data. Our second fast-track approach uses extant data, wherever possible, in performing full-scale evaluations. Under this approach, we have relied on existing federal, state, and local data to help expedite phases of the evaluation process, such as the literature review, the research design, and, of course, data collection.

Prospective Evaluation Synthesis (PES). PES, our most recent approach, is a three- to four-month "front-end" evaluation that intervenes between the time a decision is made to propose a new program and the time the program begins. PES clarifies the assumptions underlying program goals, identifies the problems to be addressed, and suggests the best intervention point and the type of intervention most likely to succeed. PES does this by bringing an understanding of the past effects of similar programs to the design and development of new ones.

Today, program evaluations are a familiar adjunct of congressional policy-making; they now figure notably in program reauthorizations, legislative decisions and markups, oversight, and informed public debate. For example, one PEMD evaluation helped working mothers leaving the Aid to Families with Dependent Children Program to receive Medicaid health insurance for their children over longer periods of time. Another set of studies held up production of the inadequately tested Bigeye bomb. Another evaluation led to doubled funding for the high-quality Runaway and Homeless Youth Program, although the relevant executive agency had proposed halving the appropriation. Another evaluation (on employee stock ownership plans) was responsible for a reduction of nearly $2 billion in tax expenditures. And another evaluation showed that an increase in the drinking age from eighteen to twenty-one unambiguously reduces traffic fatalities, spurring legislation to this effect in sixteen sites and resulting in the estimated saving of one thousand young lives in 1987 alone.

Auditors and Social Scientists

The challenge of bringing social scientists into an auditing agency was more indirect than the other challenges. It did not involve program evaluation's ability to satisfy a congressional user but rather its ability to satisfy that user while working as a component of GAO. One problem when social scientists began working with auditors was that too few in either group saw the need (or took the time) to learn about the other group's skills. Both sides tended to speak from an entrenched (and fortified) social science or auditing position without examining carefully what the position resulted from, what the real conceptual and methodological differences were between auditors and evaluators, and what similarities could be drawn upon to build a productive relationship.

Different Approaches

Just how are auditing and evaluation different? Evaluation, as I noted earlier, leans heavily on the use of research methods. Auditing, on the other hand, is a process of "objectively obtaining and evaluating evidence regarding assertions about economic actions and events to ascertain the degree of correspondence between those assertions and established criteria, and communicating the results to interested users" (American Accounting Association, 1973, p. 2). Auditing thus seeks to examine the match between a criterion and a condition (that is, the matter or "assertion" being audited). Evaluation focuses more on measuring what has occurred, estimating what would have happened without the program or policy and comparing the two situations to determine program effects.

Synergism

We discovered at GAO that once auditors and social scientists understood each other's perspectives and approaches and how they differed, opportunities for interchange and method borrowing began to appear. Evaluators, for instance, have long borrowed accounting methods to measure efficiency, especially when performing cost-benefit or cost-effectiveness analyses.

We are now seeing the program divisions of GAO publish strong evaluations, featuring an accomplished use of study design and sampling. One example is an analysis of the effect on airfares of the increasing concentration in the airline industry.

Overall, our experience of the past ten years shows that it is entirely possible for auditors and social scientists not only to share the same work place in reasonable harmony but also to learn from each other and to work together productively. With the first hurdles behind them, auditors and evaluators share many points on which to build. The work of both is typically retrospective—that is, auditors and evaluators alike have an interest in shoring up the "audit trail." Both must face up to new congressional demands for prospective work. Both follow systematic work processes, and although it is true that these differ in aim and approach, it is also true that auditors at GAO are beginning to pay more attention to the design of their projects, and that evaluators are coming to appreciate the value of auditors' mechanisms for quality control. Both are concerned that their work be useful to their sponsors and to the public. Finally, both auditors and evaluators must parry assaults on the independence of their work, and the protections that GAO's auditors have established make the organization an ideal place in which to conduct program evaluations.

What, then, can others learn from our experience? Perhaps the most important point is that, to be viable, an evaluation function needs independence, skilled personnel, users who understand the benefits to be drawn from evaluation findings, and the ability to respond appropriately to these users' information needs. When such a function exists, and findings can make their way unimpeded into the policy-making process, then evaluation can serve its true purpose: to help make government more effective.

Reference

American Accounting Association. *A Statement of Basic Auditing Concepts*. Studies in Accounting Research, no. 6. Sarasota, Fla.: American Accounting Association, 1973.

ELEANOR CHELIMSKY is assistant comptroller general, Program Evaluation and Methodology Division, General Accounting Office.

The Congressional Budget Office provides analytical advice to Congress on the development of the national budget. While its work is not strictly program evaluation, it does involve the use of analytical evaluation techniques, especially cost-effectiveness and cost-benefit analysis, based mostly on secondary data.

The Congressional Budget Office: An Emphasis on Cost-Effectiveness and Cost-Benefit Analysis

Dawn W. De Vere

In 1974, the Congressional Budget Office (CBO) was established as part of a broader effort to strengthen and support the process of developing a national budget in the Congress. While its chartered mission was defined as provision of economic and budgetary assistance to Congress, the actual scope of CBO's analytical activities is extensive, paralleling the broad range of budget topics affecting the nation's economy.

This chapter begins with a history of organizational structure and the legislative responsibilities delegated to CBO and focuses on its production of objective, politically neutral information for the budget process. Discussion then turns to specific functions of the major offices within CBO and a description of its analytical focus.

CBO does not have an organizational unit with the exclusive mission of program evaluation, nor does it specifically define its analytical work as evaluation. Nevertheless, all of its work is analytical, much of it is based on empirical studies, and a good deal of it is evaluative in nature. CBO's major evaluation activity involves secondary data, which are distilled and reanalyzed for use in development of budget estimates, economic forecasts, and program analysis and policy alternatives.

Legislative Background

CBO was instituted as an analytical support agency for the congressional budget process by the Congressional Budget and Impoundment Control Act of 1974. The intent of the act was to provide Congress with a strong and credible information base to counteract the balance of power over legislative appropriations that seemed to weigh too much in favor of the executive branch.

In establishing a new budget process, the act also created budget committees in both the Senate and the House of Representatives in an effort to impose tighter discipline in the approval of federal appropriations. The act further stipulated that CBO give equal priority to analytical work and other information requested by the budget, tax, and appropriations committees. Other congressional committees are entitled to the same budget and cost projections; however, work requests beyond the immediate scope of budget considerations are provided at a lower priority level.

In order to retain objectivity in all analyses, the agency is under a mandate to maintain a strictly nonpartisan character. Consequently, while provision of alternative policy options is a requirement, the act bars CBO from making policy recommendations. Although CBO budget estimates, economic forecasts, and cost projections are generally less optimistic than projections from the incumbent administration, CBO has earned a reputation of impartial professionalism for its provision of empirically based, credible estimations in a highly charged political environment. This reputation has enabled Congress to confidently challenge budget information presented by an administration, as well as to engage in policy debate from a more equitable position.

CBO Budget and Staff

Unlike many analytical and evaluation functions in the executive branch, budget and staffing support for CBO increased during the 1980s. In 1980, its budget was $13,586,000; ten years later it was $19,950,000, an increase of 50 percent. In the same period, CBO staff increased a modest amount from 218 to 226. When compared to the large, absolute declines in evaluation budgets and staff taking place in the executive branch, the growth of CBO's resources is even more significant.

CBO Organization and Functions

In terms of organizational structure, legislative functions are roughly divided between budget responsibilities and program analysis, with divisions following the lines of task-related support services. Although this structure guides work assignments, joint studies with other divisions are common. Frequent interaction and information pooling among CBO's divisions reinforces the efficient preparation of high-quality final products.

Under CBO's director, six assistant directors manage divisions comprising the agency's organizational base.

Tax and Budget Analyses. Divisions responsible for budget assistance and economic forecasting focus almost exclusively on synthetic evaluation functions. These range from very basic to quite sophisticated analyses, with some requiring in-house development of elaborate statistical models. There are three such divisions: Budget Analysis, Tax Analysis, and Fiscal Analysis.

The Budget Analysis Division bears responsibility for preparing the hundreds of cost estimates for legislative proposals introduced each year by congressional committees. Cost estimates also require a five-year forecast report on the probable dollar impact of each proposal on both expenditures and revenues. A running record of these tabulations is maintained by the scorekeeping unit.

In 1985, the Balanced Budget Act introduced another statutory requirement: the sequestration report intended to provide Congress with alternative strategies for meeting annual deficit reduction goals. To carry out the requirements of this act, the Budget Analysis Division prepares an annual review of the president's budget using CBO's baseline values and methodology for cost projections and economic forecasts. Annual reports to the budget committees and budget reform studies for legislative proposals are ongoing tasks.

The Tax Analysis Division focuses on review of tax expenditures and provides revenue estimates. It also prepares studies related to tax policy, examines existing tax structure, and evaluates how that design affects the budget and economy. The results of studies are essential to the development of effective alternative tax strategies.

The Fiscal Analysis Division focuses on economic forecasts and projections. Studies undertake intensive review of economic trends in areas such as employment, income, production, credit, and inflation, which are then digested and evaluated for use in projecting how present or alternative policies might affect the future economy. This work is essential to the budget committees in the formulation of resolutions on the budget. Since CBO does not have an in-house econometric model, forecasts are generally the result of a judgment process directed by staff and CBO economic advisers. Information obtained from outside forecast sources and leading econometric models aid this process.

Program Analyses. Three other divisions carry out analyses related to programs. Their work is done in response to congressional requests to evaluate likely consequences of proposed policies and programs. Their specific purpose is to calculate the probable impact of proposed policies and programs on current programs, the budget, and the economy; and to develop a range of alternatives to the proposed policy or program and provide the same types of estimations for these alternatives. The three divisions that carry out this work include Human Resources and Community Development, which prepares analyses on topics of health, education, social security, housing, social services, community development, and other related issues; Natural Resources and Commerce, which provides services to committees formulating legislation for energy, environment, agriculture, public works, industry and trade, and research development and technology; and National Security, which furnishes analyses and reports on matters concerning national defense, related expenditures, and Department of Defense programs.

Other Functions. Two other functions are linked directly to CBO's director. These are the Office of the General Council (OGC) and the Office of Intergovernmental Relations (OIGR). The OGC is responsible for the agency's legal activities, interpretation of statutes, analysis of proposed legislation, and procurement review procedures.

The OIGR has a more diverse role with three distinct functions. Its principal task is to serve as a communication link between the Congress and state and local governments, and to provide budget and policy information to nongovernment organizations, the media, and the general public. As a center for communications, all activities related to CBO publications are facilitated through this office. The office also coordinates the information-sharing network among the four congressional support agencies to avoid redundancy in studies. Representatives from each agency meet every couple of months in an ongoing effort to avert any overlap or duplication, although some studies are performed jointly. OIGR also functions as an internal management organ for CBO, furnishing the agency with all its administrative support services. Finally, evaluation functions are carried out by a program analysis unit within OIGR. This unit also examines all budget issues affecting organization or management in the federal, state, and local government sectors.

Budget and Staff. In its first year, CBO operated with a budget of just over $6 million, with its staff total limited by a statutory ceiling predetermined by annual appropriations. Between 1976 and 1991, increases in appropriations lifted that ceiling from 193 positions to 226. Total staff in 1991 stood at 218 with a $21 million appropriation.

CBO has a highly skilled staff. Most of the professional staff have bachelor's degrees, more than 70 percent have graduate degrees, and 35 percent hold doctoral degrees. Among those with graduate degrees, economists predominate, with public policy and public administration the next largest category.

Shift in Staff Allocation. In the planning stage of operations, original intentions were to assign the bulk of staff (45 percent) to the program analysis divisions, including OIGR's general government unit, while a leaner staff (30 percent) would support the tax and budget analysis divisions. The early 1980s, however, ushered in a period when preoccupation with budget pressures focused greater attention on reductions of the federal budget and the federal deficit.

The most prominent legislation to evolve at the time was the Balanced Budget and Emergency Control Act of 1985, which expanded the statutory responsibilities of CBO's tax and budget divisions. This act necessitated an early reshuffling of staff to tax and budget analysis to handle the increased workload related to national debt solutions. The result was a reduction of staff for program analysis divisions. By 1980, budget assistance received 54 percent of staff allocations, whereas only 34 percent went to program analysis.

The enactment of the Omnibus Budget Reconciliation Act of 1990 further expanded tasks with its provision of enforcing limits on discretionary spending. Today's staff assignments show a slight increase in staff for tax and budget analysis, while program analysis has experienced a decrease.

Change in Publications. CBO publications have been similarly affected by budget and time pressures. Between 1980 and 1989, there was an overall reduction in published reports and studies, with program analysis divisions experiencing the greatest decline. This trend does not, however, indicate a reduction in analytical studies since figures for the same years reveal that the number of unpublished analyses nearly doubled. Rather, legislative time constraints on budget matters have meant an increase in quick turnaround analyses and, consequently, an alteration in final form. Today, more analyses are furnished through unpublished papers, committee reports, and staff memoranda.

Evaluation Activities

Given the objectives and features of work performed at CBO, evaluation activities would seem to be a natural component of the analysis process. And, in fact, much of the work done by CBO is evaluative in nature, although it is spoken of as "analysis." For example, financial analysis involves collecting estimates for a program's total cost, impact analysis reviews program outcomes to determine overall program effectiveness against its objectives, and compliance analysis assesses costs and impact of compliance with proposed mandates for different levels of government.

The fundamental evaluation techniques used most in CBO studies are cost-effectiveness and cost-benefit analyses. Cost-effectiveness studies have been most useful when applied to existing policy for the development of alternative courses of action for output goals and projected costs for each option. In using this method, no attempt is made to measure or assign a value to a program's consumer advantage since, in certain cases, it is nearly impossible to determine outcome values (for example, national security or defense programs).

Cost-benefit analysis provides a more sophisticated approach to CBO's evaluation work. As a prescriptive model in quantitative analysis, it employs a method, or model, to estimate the outcome value in terms of dollar amount. Further, before any legislative decisions are made on the fate of proposed policy, cost-benefit studies investigate and evaluate probable impacts of the original proposal and alternatives to it.

Professional Standards Review Organization Study

The way in which CBO carries out its work can be seen in its handling of the Professional Standards Review Organization (PSRO). The analysis was designed to assess the effectiveness of evaluation methods and survey data of the PSRO program, whose stated objective was to "promote the effective, efficient, and economical delivery of health care services of proper quality." As is the case with almost all CBO analyses, no original data were collected for the project. The project was handled by CBO's Human Resources and Community Development Division. Data for the analysis were drawn from evaluations of several review organizations, simulating, in varying ways, the basic PSRO program model. In order to test the cost-effectiveness and performance of the PSRO program, three questions were formulated by CBO: How effective is the program in reducing hospital utilization? Are the savings associated with the program large enough to justify the costs of the program? Are the program's net savings large enough to warrant the expectation that PSROs will play a major role in containing health care costs?

The study revealed weaknesses in PSRO review methodology, which led to questionable data. With regard to the first question, even though reanalysis of research statistics pointed to a 2 percent reduction in the number of days that medicare project participants were under hospital care, CBO still offered the following counsel: "This estimate has to be viewed with caution, however. Most extant evaluation studies are too flawed to be reliable, and furthermore, they yield inconsistent evidence. Even the best research available—a generally sound study conducted by HEW's Health Care Financing Administration (HCFA), on which the 2 percent estimate is based—also suffers from some important weaknesses" (CBO, 1979, p. ix).

The second question produced a negative response as well. CBO reported that "reanalysis of data revealed no net savings at all," which, in effect, carried the same dismal message to the final question. Estimates indicated that high cost for long-term care would eclipse any net savings that could be attributed to the PSRO program.

CBO's overall judgment on the effectiveness of PSROs? Statistical data and prevailing sentiment provided little support for success. Suggestions were offered, however, on the program's need for reanalysis using well-structured alternatives to previously applied methodology, and for more carefully selected sampling groups. Studies such as this typically take the longest to complete; in some cases, such as the PSRO study, up to two years are necessary, whereas others are completed within a nine- to twelve-month period.

A Look at Performance Measures

Another project currently in progress at CBO is a comparative study designed to evaluate the use of performance measures at different levels of government. This project is somewhat of a departure from the customary form of agency analysis. The study, directed by OIGR's program analysis unit, runs parallel to the program performance issue presently under discussion in Congress. Since a number of federal agencies, such as the General Accounting Office and the Office of Management and Budget, have also undertaken projects dealing with issues of performance management, communication channels have been opened among agency representatives to coordinate information resources and project methodology.

CBO's unit is looking at state and local governments that have had a high rate of success for programs already testing performance measures. In comparing and evaluating the types of performance measures used in case studies, CBO is concentrating on analysis from three perspectives. The first of these examines the overall performance of a particular agency. The second viewpoint deals exclusively with measures of performance in a single department of that agency. The third perspective attempts to evaluate organizations that have met with failure in their performance measures.

Questions concern not only types of measures but also *what* is being measured, *how* it is measured, and whether the *right* things are being measured. Internal and external surveys will comprise part of the project and are devised to draw on the perceptions of those agencies conducting program performance. A typology of performance measures initiated by various government units will be compiled as well. Since this study is still underway, a final analysis of substantive information has not yet been conducted.

Finally, CBO is a major user of statistics and information from multiple outside sources, such as those collected for population surveys and national censuses, program data or analyses prepared by various federal agencies, and studies provided by independent or private-sector organizations. The quality of numerous CBO studies is dependent on the availability, accuracy, and reliability of that information base. CBO's reputation for generating accurate and objective analyses can only improve as outside data collection improves and enlarges, and the effective integration of evaluation programs and methodology regains a place of prominence.

Reference

Congressional Budget Office. *The Effects of PSROs on Health Care Costs: Current Findings and Future Evaluation.* Washington, D.C.: Government Printing Office, 1979.

DAWN W. DE VERE is a research assistant at the National Academy of Public Administration, Washington, D.C., where she is working on program evaluation and performance monitoring in the federal government.

The Congressional Research Service provides analytical work on request to members of Congress. Much of this is short-term information and background research, but some is substantial in-depth research and analysis. Analysis is almost always based on secondary data and rarely employs sophisticated methodologies.

The Congressional Research Service

Barbara Poitras Duffy

Working as an exclusive and direct research arm of Congress, the Congressional Research Service (CRS) is a department within the Library of Congress. CRS provides Congress with expert and independent assessments of national and international events, conditions, and existing laws and programs and analyzes options for change. The purpose of CRS is to inform, not to persuade, and to contribute to an informed national legislature.

CRS serves Congress in a manner consistent with the underlying characteristics of the American constitutional system and the national political process. The Constitution divides powers between the president and Congress, thereby creating "competition" for power. In order to compete effectively, Congress requires independent access to policy-related information, data, and analyses. During each stage of the legislative process, CRS is available to assist members of Congress in fulfilling their institutional and constitutional duties.

A multifaceted organization, CRS provides accurate, timely, nonpartisan services, ranging from the provision of general information to the performance of complex analytical functions. CRS provides three basic types of services: (1) information and research based on requests for facts and data, (2) analysis of legislative and policy alternatives, and (3) in-house "think tank" and more complex analyses, such as the development of econometric models. It also produces self-initiated work in anticipation of requests for information. With approximately 860 permanent staff members and a

---

The opinions expressed in this chapter are those of the author and do not necessarily represent or reflect the positions of the Federal Bureau of Investigation.

funding level of $60 million for fiscal year 1992, CRS responds to more than half a million requests per year.

Mission of CRS

In maintaining a close relationship with Congress, and in keeping with its broad congressional mandate, CRS provides a variety of services in an effort to maintain an informed national legislature. CRS works exclusively and directly for all members and committees of Congress in support of their legislature, oversight, and representational responsibilities. CRS supports the members, committees, and leaders of the House and Senate at all stages of the legislative process by responding to requests for research, analyses, and informational services that are nonpartisan and confidential.

CRS attempts to anticipate congressional analytical and research needs by projecting which major issues are likely to be addressed by each house to ensure that they have collected the appropriate information and prepared those work products that members are most likely to require. This projection helps CRS utilize its resources most efficiently and respond to the frequently short deadlines of congressional requests.

By law, CRS is not permitted to collect original data for its reports to Congress. Instead, it synthesizes materials that have already been published. This approach to information production allows CRS to respond quickly to congressional requests, thereby increasing the potential utility of the information. CRS also seeks to help requestors reduce information overload by only supplying what is requested. CRS furnishes information only to the requestor; it is not disseminated to all members of Congress or to the public.

History of CRS

The history of the organization spans nearly two centuries, dating back to 1800, when Congress established a small working library. By the early 1900s, a need was identified for a specific operation within the Library of Congress to focus on legislative issues. In 1913, the Senate Library Committee requested the establishment of a legislative reference bureau. In 1946, the service was mandated to enhance its analytical research capabilities by hiring subject area experts. In 1970, the Legislative Reference Service was renamed the Congressional Research Service and authorized to expand the research support provided to Congress.

Budget and Staffing of CRS

Over the ten-year period from 1980 to 1990, the CRS budget increased substantially from $30,335,000 to $49,806,000. Of this amount, the respective figures for policy analysis and research are $20,566,000 and $30,382,000, again a substantial increase. During the same period, staff resources for the entire organization declined from 941 to 876.

Organization of CRS

CRS is primarily staffed by professionals representing a wide range of expertise, including economists, attorneys, engineers, scientists, health care analysts, foreign affairs specialists, political scientists, educators, public administrators, and social scientists. Annually, CRS responds to half a million inquiries that encompass a wide range of issues. About two-thirds of these inquiries seek very basic facts and information, although staff members are available to perform research and analyses on any topic of interest to Congress.

CRS analysts typically present research findings orally to Congress. Senior analysts, who are nationally known experts in their fields, also produce extensive written reports. Their work is sought by media reporters as background information for fast-breaking issues. CRS work is disseminated to members of Congress or to committee staff, via briefings, seminars, and workshops, although research products may also take the form of memoranda or formal reports. Occasionally, videotapes are prepared as briefing products.

CRS has seven research divisions: American Law, Economics, Education and Public Welfare, Environment and Natural Resources Policy, Foreign Affairs and National Defense, Government, and Science Policy. The Congressional Reference Division handles requests that require reference information rather than analysis. It also administers the CRS Reference Centers and Information Distribution Centers. The Library Services Division also provides bibliographies.

When inquiries are made to CRS, the Inquiry Section staff identify the types of information or analyses needed, the format that best meets the needs of the requestor, and the deadline for the information. All requests are logged in and assigned upon receipt through a computerized system that helps to track requests. Almost half of all requests are made through the Inquiry Section; the remaining requests are submitted through the Reference Centers located in the Library of Congress and in the House and Senate office buildings.

CRS Personnel

Senior managers of CRS recruit widely for subject area experts at graduate schools in order to identify candidates for entry-level CRS positions. If individuals successfully complete the summer program (and their respective graduate programs), they may be offered permanent employment. While analytical, interpersonal, and oral communications skills are important, CRS views strong written skills as essential. CRS attributes authorship on all publications, often resulting in additional requests to specific analysts to provide further products. This system encourages specialization, professionalism, and, at the upper levels, a high degree of independence, similar to what one would find in a university setting.

CRS staff members are highly educated and trained and are promoted on the basis of merit. All analysts are provided extensive computer training on all of the software packages necessary to conduct their work. Analysts have their own computers, which help them respond to requests for multiple work products. In general, about 75 percent of their work products are turned out within forty-eight hours of the requests, and 90 percent of their work is turned out within a week, except at the senior level, where in-depth reports are prepared on specific issues. Analysts are responsible for continuously updating their work products to keep them current in anticipation of future requests. Whenever possible, they try to prepare generic information in order to respond to the greatest number of inquiries.

By law, CRS analysts are prohibited from conducting fieldwork; this responsibility belongs to the U.S. General Accounting Office (GAO). However, when necessary or appropriate, CRS coordinates studies and shares information with GAO. CRS will deny requests for information if they require fieldwork or, more appropriately, belong to another agency, such as GAO, the Office of Technology Assessment, or the Congressional Budget Office.

Senior Research Specialists and Contract Work

CRS has a cadre of senior specialists whose role is statutorily mandated. These specialists are nationally and internationally recognized experts in their fields and have extensive backgrounds outside CRS in the private sector, academia, or government. They typically respond to congressional requests for more sophisticated types of analyses, often functioning as consultants to particular committees. Senior specialists also coordinate interdivisional and interdisciplinary projects. However, if an inquiry exceeds the subject matter expertise of current senior specialists, CRS utilizes consultants who are already on contract. Most work is done in-house because the budget for external consultants is small. All contract studies are monitored by senior specialists and reviewed for compliance with CRS standards and policies.

Additional Components of CRS

CRS is also responsible for tracking significant legislative issues and identifying for Congress any issues that deserve special attention. Each January, the *CRS Review* highlights major issues of special interest to the current

Congress. It also prepares specialized "Issue Briefs" that address pertinent questions, track legislative developments, and provide a guide for all CRS work products.

The Congressional Reference Division of CRS is responsible for congressional requests for information and reference. It does not perform any original analyses. This division utilizes standard reference tools, computerized bibliographies, and Library of Congress collections to respond to requests for information. It offers quick reference services, providing liaison between congressional offices and CRS staff.

The Library Services Division offers information support services to CRS. It is responsible for securing materials and bibliographical services, as well as for reference services for the analyses assigned to the substantive research divisions. It also provides specialized services directly to Congress.

CRS employees also conduct seminars and workshops, coordinated by the Office of Special Programs, in conjunction with research analysts assigned to the substantive research divisions. Participants are members and the staffs of Congress, CRS specialists, and subject area experts. CRS also provides training in legislative research, constituent casework, and the legislative process to help congressional staffs become familiar with the wide array of available resources as well as understand congressional operations.

Audiovisual services are provided by CRS on a variety of topics of current interest to Congress. Video programs are broadcast during the week on the congressional cable system, available on most television sets on Capitol Hill. Audio briefs are also produced by CRS and present discussions on major public policy issues and programs on how Congress works.

The Language Services Section of CRS is composed of linguists, who perform a variety of services for Congress, although most requests are for written translations. This section provides services in eleven languages; when necessary, arrangements are made for translations in other languages.

Summary and Conclusion

CRS works exclusively and directly for all members and committees of the Congress in support of their legislative, oversight, and representational functions. It maintains close ties to Congress and, in keeping with its broad congressional mandate, provides a wide range of services to create an informed national legislature that is well equipped to compete in the American political process.

BARBARA POITRAS DUFFY is an evaluator assigned to the Office of Planning, Evaluation, and Audits in the U.S. Federal Bureau of Investigation.

The Office of Technology Assessment had a controversial beginning amid charges of politicization and poor-quality work. But during the 1980s a better assessment process, including broader participation by client groups and greater oversight by technical experts, led to radically improved studies.

The Analytical Work of the Office of Technology Assessment

Elizabeth A. Hildes

The Office of Technology Assessment (OTA) had a controversial beginning but has developed into a respected producer of useful analytical work on technology. This chapter begins by depicting the OTA's analytical activity during its early years, from 1972 to 1979, and continues by describing its operation from 1979 to 1992.

OTA: 1970–1979

OTA was established under the Office of Technology Assessment Act of 1972. Under this act, OTA provides Congress with assessments or studies that identify the range of likely positive and negative consequences of policy alternatives affecting the use of technology.

OTA is overseen by a bipartisan, thirteen-member Technology Assessment Board (TAB), which includes six senators appointed by the president pro tempore, six members of the House of Representatives appointed by the Speaker, and the director of OTA, who is a nonvoting member. The chair alternates between parties and branches of Congress. TAB is advised by an advisory council, the Technology Assessment Advisory Council, which is appointed by the board. The council is made up of ten public members eminent in science and technology. The comptroller general of the United States and the director of the Congressional Research Service serve as statutory members. TAB appoints the director of OTA, who serves a six year term. The president serves as a nonvoting member of TAB.

OTA is organized into three operating divisions: Energy, Materials, and International Security; Health and Life Sciences; and Science, Information, and Natural Resources. Each division is headed by an assistant director and includes topically oriented analytical groups. OTA staff are about equally balanced between engineers and scientists, on the one hand, and social scientists and lawyers, on the other. OTA has been unsuccessful in recruiting top-notch people in categories that offer only temporary appointments. Among these positions are physician, biologist, civil engineer, computer scientist/engineer, engineer with industrial experience, international economist, and systems integrator.

Budget and Staffing in the 1970s

The first appropriation for OTA was not made until 1974. The appropriation at that time totaled $2.5 million, half of the original $5 million requested. The appropriation increased to $6.8 million in 1977 but still only provided OTA with limited resources to study the range of programs assigned to it. OTA staff did not have their own space until 1978. Prior to 1978, staff worked throughout the House and Senate office buildings.

During its initial years, OTA was under constant attack for the quality of its work. Critics charged that project decisions were geared to short-term political desires of board members, that OTA duplicated research already conducted by competing federal agencies, and that some of its reports were mediocre and unimaginative.

OTA: 1979–1992

Under the present director, John Gibbons, the productivity of the agency increased, disparities between programs were reduced, quality improved, and the authority and credibility of the agency grew. Since 1979, the emphasis has been on institutionalizing the OTA process in Congress and improving OTA's methodology and management. Improvement began in 1979 when Gibbons established the officewide Task Force on Technology Assessment Methodology and Management. The mission of the task force was to identify and develop ways in which OTA could improve its methodology and management of technology assessment.

Budget and Staffing in the 1980s and Early 1990s

As OTA has improved its operations, Congress has increased its annual budget despite general reductions elsewhere in the government, especially in the executive branch. Despite the general demand for budget cuts in 1982, OTA was given an increase of 7.5 percent. In 1988, OTA received $16.5 million, and, for 1993, it has requested a budget of $23,668,000. This would be a 12.6 percent increase over fiscal year 1992. Throughout the 1980s and early 1990s, OTA has consistently had a staff of about 150 employees. The number of permanent staff members has remained small over the last decade, even though the budget has grown.

Assessment Process

The OTA assessment process developed during the 1980s has continued to the present day. It can be summarized by the following fifteen steps:

1. Project origination: consultation with committee members and staffs
2. Proposal formulation and internal review
3. TAB review and approval of study proposal
4. Planning and choosing methodologies
5. Staffing
6. Ensuring public participation
7. Selecting and convening an advisory panel
8. Data collection and analysis
9. Contracting
10. Report writing
11. Review and revision
12. OTA director and TAB approval of report
13. Publishing
14. Follow-up
15. Closeout

Project Origination. Requests for assessments can be made by the chair of any congressional committee acting for himself or herself or on behalf of a ranking minority member or a majority of committee members, by the OTA board, or by the OTA director in consultation with TAB. Individual members of Congress may not request OTA studies on their own. The OTA staff consults with key congressional staffers to select and schedule critical studies. The resulting proposal must be approved by the congressional advisory board.

Proposal Formulation and Internal Review. The project formulation process consists of two stages (Procter, 1987): (1) preparation of a ten- to twenty-page project proposal for approval by TAB and (2) preparation of a much more extensive study plan. This more complete study plan is reviewed by an advisory panel consisting of fifteen to twenty experts, stakeholders (those who will be affected by and care about the outcome of a technology issue), and players (those inside and outside of Congress who expect to influence legislative or executive action on an issue). The plan must also be acceptable to the congressional clients of the project. The study development process usually takes at least three months and can involve complicated discussions as various viewpoints are reconciled.

TAB Review and Approval of Study Proposal. Since the OTA does not have the resources to handle every request, it has developed a broad set of criteria for selecting, with TAB approval, topics from among those requested.

The following questions are used to choose topics for actual study: Is this a major national issue? Can OTA make a significant, unique contribution? Are the technological impacts irreversible? How imminent are the impacts? Is sufficient knowledge available to conduct the assessment? Can the scope of the study be bounded within reasonable limits? Can the study be conducted within the budget and time required? Consideration of these factors ensures that a study will not be undertaken as the pet project of a particular congressional representative.

Planning and Choosing Methodologies. The project's breadth and methodology are determined by the issues addressed. This process of issue definition is often complicated and continues throughout the project. The study plan, which also develops throughout the project, is the responsibility of the project director. The project director attempts to define and focus attention on a set of hypotheses early in the analysis in order to see possible links among issues, identify the most important potential policy actions, and design the research to test the impact of these actions.

Staffing and Ensuring Public Participation. Following approval of a proposal, the OTA senior staff pick a project team. This team assembles an ad hoc advisory panel of about twenty people, including subject matter experts and stakeholders. The group is usually very diverse in backgrounds. OTA's project team reads through assorted literature, lets contracts for research, and organizes workshops. During this stage, the team identifies the key issues that are of policy concern in the assessment through intense interaction with the congressional clients and the advisory panel. There is constant tension between the need to address all of the significant related issues and the need to keep the study range manageable.

Selecting and Convening an Advisory Panel. Advisory panels are essential elements of OTA studies. These panels ensure that all interests potentially affected by the outcome of the technology issue are considered in setting the goals and priorities of analysis and in determining the research questions and alternative policy scenarios presented.

During the two years it takes to produce a major report, the project's advisory panel holds several meetings. One meeting is for "midcourse correction." Other specialists review relevant chapters. A typical report can have as many as one hundred reviewers. All of the reviewers' comments and OTA responses are sent to TAB in what staff call the "monster memo." The board has ten days to decide whether the account is objective and to authorize its release.

The demand for assistance exceeds OTA's resources, and there is a growing waiting list. Some committees bypass standard procedures for approving reports and try to legislate reports into existence. A recent report on the Strategic Defense Initiative, mandated by Public Law 99-190, and a call for a study on the global warming trend are examples of this practice. OTA tries not to overextend itself. About thirty assessments are underway at any given time, and about fifteen to twenty studies are released each year.

Data Collection and Analysis. In choosing methodologies to examine each issue, the stakeholders and players have considerable influence. This is especially true in terms of moving OTA staff away from big, expensive, complicated data gathering or modeling efforts and in directing staff toward an examination of the complex, qualitative interactions among institutions. Three examples of methodologies are computer modeling, case studies, and workshops.

Computer modeling is used most often when trying out the results of different policy actions on situations about which there are considerable data. Qualitative techniques (for example, surveys, interviews, scenario-building, historical analogies, descriptive case studies, and workshops) may be used to supplement quantitative analyses.

Case studies explore the complex interactions among economic, political, social, and technical aspects of a technology issue. They also have the benefit of making the abstract concrete and making it easier for the audience to understand and remember the complex issues. In selecting case studies, OTA looks for typical situations and relies on the stakeholders and other reviewers for feedback. OTA uses case studies in at least half of its assessments.

Workshops serve several functions in OTA projects. Sometimes they are used to double check or evaluate quantitative information. The theory is that contractors working on OTA projects will be more careful with their analyses and data gathering when they know that they will be reviewed by a workshop full of experts in the subject areas. Workshops can also be helpful in trying to understand the future. Participants in workshops may construct scenarios, play what-if games, or fill out questionnaires. Successful workshops require approximately two months of advance preparation.

Contracting. Currently, OTA contracts out about half of the work required for a particular assessment study. Each year, about two thousand people from universities, private corporations, state and local governments, and federal agencies do work under contract or otherwise assist OTA in its assessments. The boundaries of the studies, the organization, the writing, and the presentation of the material are managed by OTA staff.

Report Writing. Reports average about three hundred pages and cost taxpayers an estimated $500,000. Each report is a comprehensive survey of what is known about a subject and a list of policy options. No recommendations are presented. Writing responsibility is normally with the project director and the project staff.

Review and Revision. Internal and external review of draft assessment reports are strongly emphasized at OTA. Internal reviewers include the program and divisional management and, when appropriate, selected OTA staff from other program areas with an interest in or perspective on the subject at hand. External review involves the OTA project advisory panel and a variety of other individuals and organizations with an interest in the subject matter. Typically, external reviewers consist of government agencies, private-sector stakeholders, public interest groups, and independent researchers and policy analysts.

OTA Director and TAB Approval of Report. The final draft of every OTA assessment report is given to the OTA director for review and, if approved, is forwarded to TAB for its review. TAB review normally takes ten working days while Congress is in session, after which, if there are no objections, the report is approved for release subject to final editing.

The authorization for release of a study indicates that TAB is satisfied that proper and accepted procedures have been followed in obtaining approval for a study proposal and its budgeting, that the advisory panel for the study has functioned properly., and that the principles of objectivity and neutrality have been upheld.

Publishing. Once TAB approves a study for release, OTA assessment reports are distributed to the requesting committees, with summaries provided to all members of Congress.

Follow-Up. The completion of an OTA report indicates the beginning of the project follow-up to communicate key findings to both the requesting congressional committee(s) and other committees that might have an interest in or jurisdiction over the topic. Requesting committees may participate in the public release of OTA reports, either through an OTA press release or a committee press release. These releases summarize the main themes of a report. Project staff are encouraged by OTA to conduct informal or formal committee briefings and present testimony on the study results, when requested.

Closeout. After a study has been completed and the report published and released, project directors are asked to prepare a closeout memo. These memos summarize who used the report and how, press coverage, follow-up requests and activities, observations on assessment methodology, and the like.

Procedures When Dealing with Classified Information

Only about 5 percent of OTA work explores classified areas, but it is often the most controversial. In 1988, OTA put together a report on the Strategic Defense Initiative. This controversial report brought substantial attack from the Pentagon. There is no clear procedure for congressional bodies in negotiating classification problems with the executive branch. The declassification review of the nine-hundred-page Star Wars report took nine months. According to OTA Director Gibbons, the delay was for political and not technical reasons.

Another sensitive study was done in 1985 on control of nuclear weapons. OTA submitted the proposal to the Joint Chiefs of Staff because of unusual security concerns. It was classified at a higher level than the top-secret clearance approved for the OTA researchers. The Pentagon consequently took the draft before anyone in Congress read it.

Conclusion

The OTA has come a long way since its inauspicious early years. Currently, it has the reputation of being the smallest and best agency for analytical work in the legislative branch. It has struggled to stay away from political influence and has become an important source of information on science and technology. In addition, OTA has developed a process that encourages diverse ideas and the use of expert information and evaluation.

Its strength is rooted in its emphasis on a participatory, iterative process. Through frequent interaction with congressional staff, OTA takes technical information and organizes and presents it in ways that help answer congressional representatives' questions and make them aware of what is policy relevant. OTA has improved the oversight function of Congress, and it has saved taxpayer dollars by pointing out to Congress more economical paths to desired goals.

Reference

Procter, M. "Probing the Core of Controversy: Issue Management in the Office of Technology Assessment." Paper presented at the European Congress on Technology Assessment, Amsterdam, The Netherlands, February 2–4, 1987.

ELIZABETH A. HILDES is a research assistant at the National Academy of Public Administration, Washington, D.C.

The GAO's transition report to the executive and legislative branches of government, Program Evaluation Issues, *began with the section "Why Program Evaluation Is Important," which is reprinted in Chapter Two of this volume. The report concluded with several sections outlining what would be needed for agencies in the executive branch to rebuild evaluation capacity and what would happen if they do not. The sections constitute a fitting conclusion to this volume.*

Rebuilding Capacity

General Accounting Office

Throughout many federal agencies the information pipeline for program oversight and management is drying up. The reduction in staff and funds needed to determine program effectiveness leaves managers unprepared to answer tough questions about program costs and results, and vulnerable to incidents such as the Vincennes situation in the Persian Gulf. Top-management support for collecting this information and insistence on honest reporting are urgently needed.

What Is Needed: Capacity

The infrastructure—the capacity for program evaluation—has generally eroded and will have to be rebuilt. For example,

Staff who are professionally trained in evaluation techniques and who also have the requisite understanding of programs will have to be recruited and trained in federal procedures. Graduate training is usually a minimum requirement for these positions.

Many evaluation units may be inadequately staffed. As a rough estimate, one evaluator can manage about $1 million in contract activity and one manager is needed for every six or seven evaluators, depending on the size and complexity of a program.

Locating at least one evaluation unit at the top-management level is essential, so that priorities can directly reflect agency and congressional concerns and the results can flow without censorship to the top.

This chapter is from U.S. General Accounting Office, *Program Evaluation Issues,* November 1988 (GAO/OCG-89-8TR).

Relationships that support planning and budget functions also need to be strengthened.

What Is Needed: Resources

A notable imbalance persists in executive branch funding of program evaluation. Some agencies say they do not do any evaluations. In others, such costly programs as Clean Water lack adequate data on program effectiveness. Given the resources that can be saved through sound evaluation and the need for an agency to be able to show that its programs are effective and well managed,

Program evaluation needs to be generally strengthened throughout the government, and

Resources need to be both dedicated to program evaluation and expanded in those agencies where evaluation has been eroded or is not functioning well.

Program evaluation personnel can present a tempting target to budget cutters in times of tight resource constraints, simply because they are not line staff. This temptation must be resisted.

What Is Needed: Priorities

Within the four areas we examined in depth, we believe the top-priority evaluation issues for the next few years are:

Integrity of weapon system evaluation,
Long-term medical care needs,
Cost-effectiveness of environmental systems, and
Excellence and competitiveness of U.S. education.

Top leadership in all agencies should review their program evaluation efforts to determine what areas in their programs need highest priority attention.

What Is Needed: Honest Reporting

Some of the problems with agency evaluations have included the failure to conduct necessary studies, nontechnical influence on draft reports that have concealed or distorted findings, technical flaws affecting study quality, the uncertain access of top managers to complete and unvarnished study findings, and the limited use of evaluations in making policy. Needed improvements in the reporting and use of program evaluation include

Assurance that objective data get to top decision makers. The review process that helps ensure technical adequacy and balance should not deter timeliness or candor.

More extensive communication between requesters and evaluators in the early, middle, and late stages of a study. Such communication, which includes evaluator participation in the early formulation of data requests, is lacking, particularly in studies mandated by Congress. Communication is crucial to keeping results of costly studies off some dusty shelf and putting them onto agendas for action.

Greater attention to the prospective aspect of evaluations, before new programs, policies, or regulations are launched. "Front end" evaluations can prevent a poor use of funds and target resources where they are most likely to be effective.

If Agencies Don't, Others Will

A consequence of the drawdown in evaluation capacity is that agencies may find themselves fenced off from evaluation-based debates about their own programs. That is, not only may agency-generated information for the public be lacking, but agencies themselves may not have the data needed to be most convincing about what they think should be started, what they think should be stopped, and what they think should be changed. The terms of the debates and the data brought to bear on these issues may be someone else's call.

Further, the problems we have described mean that to a growing extent, even GAO and others that often draw on agency records and data may be able to report little more than "Information to answer this key question is not available." That is, the loss of program evaluation information has repercussions that go beyond whether an agency head has to testify, "My Department does not have any data on that point," to whether a wide range of groups that rely in part on federally collected evaluations can independently tell Congress that is happening in the executive branch.

Over the years, the Congressional appetite for the data needed for oversight on complex questions about the operations and consequences of federal programs has not slackened. Congress increasingly is relying on GAO and its sister agencies—the Congressional Budget Office (CBO), the Office of Technology Assessment (OTA), and the Congressional Research Service (CRS)—to do studies that might appropriately be conducted by executive branch agencies. We have, for example, been tasked legislatively with a major set of analyses on the effect of immigration reform and with determination of the numbers of homeless children and youth. Clearly, if the executive branch cannot provide timely, relevant, technically adequate, and credible information on the programs that it is responsible for administering, Congress will continue to write us into legislation that mandates these important studies.

Our mission, of course, is to provide credible information to Congress and help ensure that Congress is not limited to reports from special interest, public interest, or other groups. However, although Congress may have the high ground on information, we should not, and indeed cannot, do it all.

Such a role exceeds our resources. Moreover, it could lead to a serious imbalance between the branches on who calls the shots on the information that has become a vital influence in major debates on national policy and that is considered an important indicator of a credible government.

Each agency head should have, as a top priority, an honest inventory of what information is coming on line, whether it will be available in time to affect key decisions over the next four years, what the technical quality and relevance of the evaluations are, and what gaps need to be plugged first. In a few instances, the situation may be relatively good; but in many others, we must emphasize that a renewed commitment to program evaluation is urgently needed.

INDEX

Ordering Information

New Directions for Program Evaluation is a series of paperback books that presents the latest techniques and procedures for conducting useful evaluation studies of all types of programs. Books in the series are published quarterly in spring, summer, fall, and winter and are available for purchase by subscription as well as by single copy.

Subscriptions for 1992 cost $48.00 for individuals (a savings of 20 percent over single-copy prices) and $70.00 for institutions, agencies, and libraries. Please do not send institutional checks for personal subscriptions. Standing orders are accepted.

Single copies cost $15.95 when payment accompanies order. (California, New Jersey, New York, and Washington, D.C., residents please include appropriate sales tax.) Billed orders will be charged postage and handling.

Discounts for quantity orders are available. Please write to the address below for information.

All orders must include either the name of an individual or an official purchase order number. Please submit your order as follows:

Subscriptions: specify series and year subscription is to begin
Single copies: include individual title code (such as PE1)

Mail all orders to:

Jossey-Bass Publishers
350 Sansome Street
San Francisco, California 94104

For sales outside of the United States contact:

Maxwell Macmillan International Publishing Group
866 Third Avenue
New York, New York 10022

Other Titles Available in the
New Directions for Program Evaluation Series
William R. Shadish, *Editor-in-Chief*

PE54 Evaluating Mental Health Services for Children, *Leonard Bickman, Debra J. Rog*
PE53 Minority Issues in Program Evaluation, *Anna-Marie Madison*
PE52 Evaluating Programs for the Homeless, *Debra J. Rog*
PE51 Evaluation and Privatization: Cases in Waste Management, *John G. Heilman*
PE50 Multisite Evaluations, *Robin S. Turpin, James M. Sinacore*
PE49 Organizations in Transition: Opportunities and Challenges for Evaluation, *Colleen L. Larson, Hallie Preskill*
PE48 Inspectors General: A New Force in Evaluation, *Michael Hendricks, Michael F. Mangano, William C. Moran*
PE47 Advances in Program Theory, *Leonard Bickman*
PE46 Evaluating AIDS Prevention: Contributions of Multiple Disciplines, *Laura C. Leviton, Andrea M. Hegedus, Alan Kubrin*
PE45 Evaluation and Social Justice: Issues in Public Education, *Kenneth A. Sirotnik*
PE44 Evaluating Training Programs in Business and Industry, *Robert O. Brinkerhoff*
PE43 Evaluating Health Promotion Programs, *Marc T. Braverman*
PE42 International Innovations in Evaluation Methodology, *Ross F. Conner, Michael Hendricks*
PE41 Evaluation and the Federal Decision Maker, *Gerald L. Barkdoll, James B. Bell*
PE40 Evaluating Program Environments, *Kendon J. Conrad, Cynthia Roberts-Gray*
PE39 Evaluation Utilization, *John A. McLaughlin, Larry J. Weber, Robert W. Covert, Robert B. Ingle*
PE38 Timely, Lost-Cost Evaluation in the Public Sector, *Christopher G. Wye, Harry P. Hatry*
PE37 Lessons from Selected Program and Policy Areas, *Howard S. Bloom, David S. Cordray, Richard J. Light*
PE36 The Client Perspective on Evaluation, *Jeri Nowakowski*
PE35 Multiple Methods in Program Evaluation, *Melvin M. Mark, R. Lance Shotland*
PE34 Evaluation Practice in Review, *David S. Cordray, Howard S. Bloom, Richard J. Light*
PE33 Using Program Theory in Evaluation, *Leonard Bickman*
PE32 Measuring Efficiency: An Assessment of Data Envelopment Analysis, *Richard H. Silkman*
PE31 Advances in Quasi-Experimental Design and Analysis, *William M. K. Trochim*
PE30 Naturalistic Evaluation, *David D. Williams*
PE29 Teaching of Evaluation Across the Disciplines, *Barbara Gross Davis*
PE28 Randomization and Field Experimentation, *Robert F. Boruch, Werner Wothke*
PE27 Utilizing Prior Research in Evaluation Planning, *David S. Cordray*
PE26 Economic Evaluations of Public Programs, *James S. Catterall*